Unified Integrative Medicine

A new Holistic model for personal growth and spiritual evolution

Dr. Nader Butto

authorHOUSE®

AuthorHouse™ UK
1663 Liberty Drive
Bloomington, IN 47403 USA
www.authorhouse.co.uk
Phone: 0800.197.4150

Published by AuthorHouse 04/07/2015

ISBN: 978-1-4969-9849-1 (sc)
ISBN: 978-1-4969-9850-7 (hc)
ISBN: 978-1-4969-9851-4 (e)

Print information available on the last page.

Contents

Introduction

The method presented in this book was born out of twenty-five years of experience, real dedication, study, close observation, and constant meditation on many challenging problems that the conventional biomedical system could not give clear answers to. I could perceive from the very beginning of my studies in medical school that the biomedical system has no concrete model to imply or theory to follow, and in the existing method, there are many missing points and many confusing issues for which I was seeking intuition and illumination from the ancient masters of knowledge.

Eventually, after intensive research, study, observation, and application, I was able to fit many important pieces in the right place in the puzzle. The whole picture was clearer than ever. Many missing links, one by one, began to illuminate with time. I concluded that to describe human nature, we must take into consideration the different components of the whole human being. It did not take me long to understand that physics, especially quantum mechanics, is indispensable to understanding the whole picture of the human being, especially the relationship between energy and matter. This is a main issue in resolving the missing link between mind and physical body and the dilemma of the nature of soul, its interaction with the body to generate life, and its interaction with the brain to generate the psyche. I started to study physics in order to understand better the laws of physics, and then I realized that many of the main questions that bothered me have no answers in physics either. I discovered many missing points and confusing issues precluded me from resolving them. In time, I found myself involved in research and, with real dedication, was trying to solve challenging problems that modern physics was facing. I tried to understand basic issues in order to have a whole vision that could help me to define better health and be able to heal illnesses, cure disease, and achieve a state of well-being.

When I started using the seventh sense as a method of ESP (extrasensory perception), I was able to diagnose energy blockages that caused ailments and physical disease. Upon restoring the energy balance, the physical ailment disappeared almost immediately, but after a given time, it returned. One day, while I was doing the energy balance with a woman who had been suffering for more than three years from severe and frequent abdominal pains, she started having strong emotional reactions (she laughed without apparent reason) while her whole body trembled. At the end of the therapeutic session, her pains had disappeared and she felt renewed, to such an extent that her pains never reappeared.

I saw similar reactions with other individuals but was unable to understand why it happened only to some of them. However, most of the people who had such strong reactions were completely cured after a single therapeutic session. What I actually observed was that this reaction was a strong emotional discharge related to some remote conflict from the past. From all this, I learned to understand a new aspect of the human entity, that is, the emotional one, and in consequence, I developed two new techniques.

I have called the first "Energy Emotion washout." This technique consists in giving a large quantity of energy with the hands, passing them over the whole body until physical signals of this passage appear, such as trembling, convulsions, or shivering, sometimes accompanied by emotional explosions in the form of shouting, weeping, laughing, etc. In fact, with this technique, one can clean the blocked emotions (not appropriately processed) in the soul (unconscious), which express themselves as an emotional explosion.

The second technique is that of "blinking technique," with which one can diagnose not only the specific conflict responsible for the disease of a given organ but even establish in which year and month it took place. This technique allowed me to establish the transtemporal relation between the conflict and the physical disease. The blinking technique allowed me to develop the Seventh Sense by which I could enter to the quantum realm where space and time has no meaning, and all information from past, present and future is viable.

Thanks to patients suffering from so-called "psychogenic" impotence and homosexual patients, I discovered the presence of two "major" energy poles in the human body, which are respectively located in the chest and in the abdomen. These are responsible for certain attractions or rejections in actual social intercourse and certain disturbances in the sexual behavior, specifically regarding the phenomenon of homosexuality. These poles are fed with energy provided by the parents, each one in the corresponding pole, clearly showing the relation between the affection received from parents and the homosexuality phenomenon. Thus, this discovery contrasts with and contests the theory that postulates the genetic origin of this disturbance. The energy contents of these poles is very important and establishes the level of overall vitality, because they are considered to be the generator supplying the driving force of vital energy throughout the body and the meridians.

Four phases of life allow me to understand the relationship between emotional expression and energy blockage. The four phases of life, like the four seasons, should flow continuously from one season to the other to permit the development of life. Let us imagine that the earth stopped turning around its axis and around the sun; this would be the end of our existence on earth. Life is incompatible with a single season; the face pointing to the sun would be too hot and would lead to drought, while the other face would be an endless night designed to freeze any form of life. In the same way, life is incompatible with a single stage of the cardiac cycle. The earth ceasing to rotate would be equivalent to a cardiac arrest. For life to exist, it needs to go successively through the four stations, which would be equivalent to the four stages of life: stimulation, expansion, contraction, and relaxation. Partial arrest in any of these four stages is manifested as a disease, while total arrest is tantamount to death.

The four stages of life allowed me to understand the relationship between the psyche and the physical body, such as for example a loving glance leads to an accelerated beating of the heart or the woman who for forty years wept over the loss of two sons and got a bilateral cancer in her ovaries.

I was able to see this more clearly, in particular when I understood the real function of the brain and its relation to the psyche. The brain operates like a TV set (i.e., it is a wave decoder). The interaction between the waves of the soul and the brain are analyzed and transformed into ideas, remembrances, and imagination. The memory is actually recorded as waves in the cloud of the soul. The energy of the soul has specific correspondences in the physical body. Both the soul and physical body have common points of connection in the brain. Each organ has a specific area in the brain. The organ and the related area in the brain resonate with a very specific frequency in the soul. The energy consumed during exaggerated expression of emotions is sucked in by the specific corresponding organs (sons—ovaries); however, this always passes through the brain.

More attention or concern has been given to negative and positive emotions, their natural reactions, and the damaging effect their inhibition can bring about, on the one hand, causing diseases linked to an increase in tension or stress. On the other hand, excessive expression of emotions can cause a decrease in vital energy, which is the basis of cellular degeneration, and thus cause the development of malignant diseases, such as cancer.

The relationship between the type of disease, the organ affected, and the specific conflict causing the disease is one that offers supreme clinical-practical interest, and its application is considered an enormous potential not only on a therapeutic level but also as a preventive means.

The use of energy perception through the blinking technique (seventh sense) allows me to explore the information stored in the soul, analyze it, and discover the kind of conflict the person had and the time when he or she had it. It allows us to establish, almost unequivocally, the transtemporal relation between the psychological conflict, the energy blockage, the manifestation of symptoms due to a functional unbalance, and finally the full manifestation of the organic disease.

Another therapeutic techniques such as FEEL (fast emotional elaboration and liberation) and TTRT (Trans Temporal Regression Technique) were developed in a such way that a new paradigm was born, an integrative systemic medicine that allows to free the body from ailments, allows the psyche to elaborate adequately the past conflicts and to complete the learning process and leaads the evolution of the soul.

It is important however to emphasize that healing a sick person does not only mean applying certain techniques or massages. This process makes no sense at all without patience, affection, and love for one's neighbor and for the whole universe. Technique *per se* without the human spirit would make us into machines, which we are not yet.

The Need for a New Model of Medicine

There is no doubt that conventional medicine has made tremendous achievements in emergency and trauma treatment and succeeded in prolonging life and significantly reducing mortality due to serious illnesses, such as infectious diseases and heart attacks, using life-saving treatments and operations.

The biomedical model has been a spectacularly successful model for about 150 years, so much so that it is not overtly described at all. The success of biomedicine has resulted in a shift in the burden of illness from acute infectious disease to chronic, often stress-related degenerative disease, the causes of which are largely a result of personal attitudes and lifestyles. Furthermore, medicine has advanced tremendously with the introduction of noninvasive diagnostic methods and molecular engineering (molecular) medicine.

Although biomedicine is well equipped to diagnose and treat these diseases, which are currently the major source of premature death and morbidity, its therapies rarely result in cure.

It has allowed the identification, classification, and rational treatment of a huge number of diseases; the International Classification of Disease Issue 10 (ICD-10) is the culmination of the process. Therefore, the Western biomedical system has evolved in many fields, especially in technology and biomedical research.

However, there are many ways in which it is no longer an adequate model of illness; in fact the technological progress is not associated with better understanding of the human being as a whole; it is reductionist and fails to recognize the multifactorial and mathematically complex nature of most illness.

The actual biomedical model of conventional medicine has failed gravely in the treatment and prevention of chronic illnesses. These diseases can be disabling and reduce a person's quality of life, especially if left undiagnosed or untreated. The number of people with chronic conditions is rapidly increasing; indeed, it is expected that by 2025, 50 percent of Americans will be affected by at least one chronic disease.

Only a fraction of our budget is spent on prevention and health promotion, despite evidence that prevention can do much to reduce the burden of chronic disease.

According to the Centers for Disease Control and Prevention (CDC) in the United States, 70 percent of all deaths are due to chronic disease, such as heart disease, stroke, cancer, chronic respiratory diseases, and diabetes, and the cost of chronic care exceeds $1.5 trillion a year, or 75 percent of all medical expenses.

The United States spends significantly more on health care than any other nation. In 2006, the US health-care expenditure was over $7,000 per person,[1] more than twice the average of twenty-nine other developed countries. It would cost less than ten dollars per person for prevention (see *Power of Prevention in Integrative Medicine* (2009)).

Obviously, conventional medicine did not manage to reduce the frustration from the rapid increase of chronic diseases.

What is the cause of this failure?

The characteristics that have been responsible for biomedicine's many accomplishments by necessity also define its limits. Therefore, for all its victories, conventional Western medicine hides its troubles.

Modern medicine is based upon reductionism, wherein psychology and sociology are reducible to biology, biology is reducible to chemistry, and finally chemistry is reducible to physics. According to this principle, life is defined as a sequence of chemical reaction in a solution within the cell. This approach led to the obsessive search for physical causes of disease, like microbes, gene mutation, and biochemical dysfunction. Therefore, the majority of chronic diseases, like colitis, arthritis, ulcers, heart disease, cancer, and many others, were left without known causes and therefore without real solutions for effective cures. Instead, medicine is based on clinical pharmaceutical drugs, which are not curative but only palliative, with the danger of side effects.

It is inhuman and supertechnological, and its outline is such that the physician gets increasingly farther from the patient, staying behind sophisticated instruments. The number of diseases is ever increasing, and the system in general attacks the symptom without looking for the root, thus bringing no actual cure for the disease. We get to the onset of chronic diseases, which bring along a loss of functional capacity at the individual level and an excessive burden at the socioeconomic level.

This is the result of the current understanding of illness, which is linear and reductionist. It assumes that all illness starts with a biochemical disorder within the body, causing bodily symptoms that lead to disability and restrictions on social life.

The biomedical system went out from its original path; we converted medicine to dogma with rigid rules that led us to forget the real reason why we apply medicine. It becomes the purpose instead to be the mean to prevent disease and regain health.

Therefore, we recognize the failure of the actual health model and the need for another model based on health and healing, which is efficacious and cost-effective. In order to find such a model, we need to change our thinking direction.

These are some of the reasons why people are desperately searching for real solutions, which biomedical Western medicine has not been able to achieve. It is the same reason for the increasing popularity of complementary and alternative medicine.

Therefore, today, we have two therapeutic approaches: conventional medicine and alternative complementary medicine. Both are oriented for attaining health but differ in their philosophical bases. In recent decades, integrative medicine has emerged, which involves combining conventional medicine with unorthodox treatments.

Most of the integrative medicine models proposed are more combination than integration. Nonetheless, the integration was intended to be done by pairing and integrating the latest innovations in science and medicine with the conventional deep insight of ancient healing practices that are not part of orthodox medicine and complementary medicine as currently defined or of alternative medicine (two concepts that are not synonymous but have the same therapeutic significance). Patients have more information today about their diseases and treatment options than ever before. Nevertheless, they have not had tools to help them decide among these various options, and doctors have not had the tools to gauge how acceptable an option might be to a specific patient. As a result, the medical decision made, in hindsight, may not have been the most suitable one.

What kind of model we need?

The ideal therapeutic system should be based on a holistic model that is systemic, wherein multiple biological, psychological, and social factors are seen as interlinked. Such a model should be effective in bringing back the state of well-being with minimal cost. It will restore the flow of vital energy, enhance the strength of constitution, and increase the ability of the individual to fulfill the tasks of his or her path and give him or her a sense of fulfillment and happiness. An effective therapeutic system will produce solid, reliable, and verifiable results and should be simple and readily accessible to all members of the population.

We need a model that necessarily includes public education, emphasizing disease prevention and measuring its efficacy by not only increasing life expectancy but also improving quality of life, accelerating the recovery and healing, and helping the individual obtain physical, psychological, and social well-being. In order to do that, we need to redefine the basic concepts on which health is based. We need to take into consideration the psychological aspect and its influence on physical disease; therefore, we need to redefine *psyche*. Moreover, we need to redefine *soul* or *spirit* and its influence on the physical body and the brain. We need to redefine *homeostasis*, taking into consideration the relationship between energy and matter, soul and body. To do so, we will use scientific language based on the concept of wave interference, resonance, and dissonance. The concept of health is viewed with a new-old perspective. Fortunately, the World Health (WHO) definition of health is meant to do so. It states: "Health is a state of complete physical, mental and

social wellbeing and not merely the absence of disease or infirmity"
(Introduction to the Constitution of the World Health Organization
1948).

However, in order to do so, we need a holistic model. Holism refers to
an approach to health that acknowledges that it depends upon many
interrelated components that interact in such a way that the overall
effect constitutes health (or illness).

The holistic well-being model recognizes the body, psyche, and soul
as an integrated and coherent whole. It requires a new vision of reality
that is based upon the relation between energy and matter, integrating
relativity and quantum mechanics.

Many of the alternative and complementary medicines based upon
holistic health care are perceived to be good, both morally and
practically, and refer to an approach to analyzing illness and providing
health care that acknowledges and responds to all factors relevant to the
health (or illness) of a person. However, the term itself does not signify
what those factors are or how they are classified; therefore, it is difficult
to find either any clear enunciation of what constitutes holistic health
care or any clear explanation of its practical utility.

I was lucky not to be a physicist and to feel completely free of the previous
models and dogmas accepted in physics, which could limit the imagination
and block unacceptable intuitions. I found myself involved in searching
a unified model that could be unifying physics with spirituality, modern
technology with ancient wisdom, and mathematics with philosophy.
I started to look for a theory that would describe a broad variety of
phenomena using a few arbitrary parameters. It also had to be capable of
positively predicting the results of future observation as defined by one
of the greatest philosophers of modern science, Carl Popper.

This kind of theory should be as simple as possible, so that everybody
can understand. I always thought that it should be one universal

principle, a blueprint of the universal creation that would guide its function and structure. I describe in my book *Seven Universal Principles and the Seventh Sense* the entire universe as a whole with seven simple laws. These laws are applicable to all levels of our existence, from the micro subnuclear to the macro of the galaxies and the universe itself. A unifying theory is roused up; it is called the universal unifying theory. From this theory, we constructed a new model for integrated medicine based on general laws and principles that support and guide the empirical data and experimental results. With these laws, we can define the different components of the human body, psyche, and soul using a scientific language based on accepted physical concepts. With this, we define health and the state of well-being, homeostasis, suffering, and disease. In doing so, we have created a new comprehensive rational health system, readily verifiable by actual clinical results, that can affect radical cures and help people regain the state of well-being whenever that is possible. Using these simple principles, people will generally be able to evaluate and judge the therapeutic method as to its curative mechanism and thus to take advantage of the best methods that can lead to the most efficacious possibilities.

Therefore, in this book, I propose a holistic model based on universal laws described by the unified universal theory. Through this model, we will examine the biomedical model and CAM integrative medicine to create one comprehensive model that describe our external material reality with the internal reality of emotions, thoughts, dreams, and spirits.

So, How Do We Integrate?

We need a psychosocial-bioenergetics approach based on a holistic model recognizing the whole person as physical body, psyche, and soul. We should explore, therefore, these realms as a unified model. In this model, we add psychology to medicine and spirituality to psychology. Health care should be person-centered, focusing the attention on the patient as an individual with unique biological terrain and with a special psychological temperament that leads to specific emotional crises and learning potentials. The patient takes a significant part in the process of treatment and recovery with full cooperation. The physician/practitioner shares data and doubts in order to give the solution best suited to him or her, while taking into account the condition of his or her mind and his or her fears and feelings, helping him or her to find the relationship between emotional crises and physical diseases. The functional illnesses (so-called nonorganic), which are common but still not well-managed in health-care systems, take a central importance, as they are considered as early signs of future diseases. Therefore, when well-managed, this model leads to organic disease prevention.

The physical body is checked and examined as in the biomedical system, centered on organs and physiological functions; the psyche is explored by examining behavior, life style, stress, emotional crises, and social-role function. The soul is examined based on new quantum physics concepts, such as quantum potential and quantum states, in order to explain the soul as an energy phenomenon. This explains the meaning of spiritual needs, such self-realization and personal fulfillment, focusing on choice (free will) and quality of life.

In order to do so, we must explore the advantages and disadvantages of conventional and unconventional medicine, exploiting the advantages of each method to find a holistic diagnostic and therapeutic model that will meet the individual's emotional, social, and spiritual needs and coordinate the scientific and technological development with these needs, in order to obtain the best of both from which to form unified integrative medicine into one holistic model.

Conventional Medicine

There is no doubt that conventional medicine has made tremendous achievements in emergency and trauma care and indeed, has reached impressive achievements in advancing the level of public health. The accepted indices for examining the level of health, according to the Western approach, are life expectancy and infant mortality. Indeed, life expectancy has risen as a result of the significant decline in mortality due to serious illnesses, such as infectious diseases and heart attacks, using improved CPR (cardiopulmonary resuscitation) and life-saving operations. Conventional medicine significantly enhanced the quality of life of diabetics, prolonged the life of cancer patients whose disease was discovered at the early stages, and attained considerable improvement in the incidence of infant mortality. We therefore have no doubt of the contribution of conventional medicine and can note its advantages as follows:

- Conventional medicine based on the modern scientific approach employs scientific tools and is open to evaluation and scientific examination of the effectiveness of its methods.
- Conventional medicine examines and adjusts itself, constantly innovates, and progresses in the quality of its treatments.
- Conventional medicine is the accepted method based on accepted scientific methods and can alleviate the suffering caused by various diseases. It treats the patient with greater success than any other medicine.

- Conventional medicine follows explicit and particularly cautious rules pertaining to approving medication and new methods of treatment and conducting clinical trials. Medical institutions have set clear and explicit rules of ethics regarding the doctor's obligations, medical negligence, deceiving patients, and so on.

Nevertheless, conventional medicine is limited in many areas.

The Weaknesses of Conventional Medicine

There are weaknesses in conventional medicine that are worth discussing in order to improve the treatment of the patient for the benefit of the individual and the population in general. The basic fundamental assumption made by most people is that all illness in an individual can be traced back to some specific, usually single, disorder of a part of the body. This is termed the *disease*; it refers to some distinct abnormality in structure and/or function of a single organ or organ system. It is also known as the pathology. The disorder is assumed to be within the body.

Conventional medicine assesses the person's health according to objective parameters that can be measured, such as body temperature, pulse rate, breathing rate, and blood pressure—biochemical tests of the blood and other laboratory tests. Thus, for example, high blood pressure is treated with medication in order to attain normal values, without trying to assess the environmental conditions, including emotional and mental stress caused by family conflicts, work difficulties, economic crises, and so on. Bronchial asthma is treated by bronchial dilators, without assessing the emotional condition that provokes overexcitability of the airways to external environmental stimuli, such as air contamination or cold, or internal stimuli, such as acute stress. Another assumption is that people have two parts to their existence—the physical and the mental—and that these aspects of a person are separate and unrelated. The person's body and consciousness are considered as two separate entities. This is a common belief, most obviously demonstrated in the almost universal separation between "mental" health services and "physical" health services.

Disease within the body is caused externally; the person who is ill is assumed to be the passive victim of the disorder and not responsible for his or her illness. Therefore, the treatments are an external intervention that will cure the disease, and the patient remains a passive recipient of treatment with only a minor role to play, if any.

Therefore, there is no doubt today that conventional medicine has failed gravely in the treatment and prevention of chronic illnesses. Most of the diseases from which the population suffers, such as high blood pressure, diabetes, high cholesterol, rheumatism, and advanced cancer, are chronic and have no real cure.

All the new medication and advanced technology have not prevented the development of these diseases; moreover, there is a consequent constant rise in their incidence and the rate of mortality. Cancer is just an example of this.

Despite considerable effort and the investment of hundreds of millions of dollars, the death rate from cancer is increasing. Researchers from the British Cancer Foundation published a report in April 2005 showing that the number of cases of lung and of breast cancer has doubled in the last three decades. The American Cancer Association published a report in 2005 finding that cancer held first place as a cause of death in the United States.

Lung cancer is the leading cause of death among all types of cancer, and the rate of morbidity is constantly increasing. About one million people die of lung cancer globally each year. Almost half the patients who were diagnosed and treated at the early stages of the disease, prior to its spread beyond the lungs, lived for five years or more, but according to the data of the American Cancer Association, this group of patients is only about 13 percent of all lung cancer patients.

In Israel, too, the number of cancer patients is constantly increasing. The increase in the rate of cancerous growths is not related to the rate of population growth, as some claim. In the twenty years between 1982 and 2002, the number of residents of Israel grew by 63 percent, while the growth in the number of cancer incidents diagnosed in those years was 140 percent. Between 1975 and 2002, the number of new patients grew from 214 to 301 per annum for every 100,000 residents, an increase of 40 percent. The probability of an Israeli having cancer was formerly 1:3, and now, it is 1:2.5.

The mortality rate from malignant illnesses has hardly changed in the last twenty years. Therefore, the benefit of prolonging life through treating these illnesses is marginal, despite the tremendous investment in identifying and treating them.

In the last twenty years, the life expectancy of the Western population has increased by six years. The main life prolongation (3.9 years) was attained because of the decline in death from heart disease, blood vessel diseases, and cerebrovascular diseases, such as brain hemorrhage. But such a decline in the mortality rate is accompanied by an increasing number of people living with damage to the affected organs, such as congestive heart failure, physical limitations, postcerebral hemorrhage, or kidney failure. These people live for many more years with an extremely poor quality of life and significant limitations to their physical, emotional, and social functioning.

Therefore, we can point out the disadvatages of the conventional medicine:

- According to the Western biomedical model, health is measured on the basis of quantitative statistical data, focusing mainly on the symptoms and only rarely relating importance to prevention or to the cause of the disease. The main purpose of Western medicine is to eradicate the symptoms, not necessarily worrying about achieving full physical, emotional, and social well-being.

Therefore, Western medicine does not imply the concept of "health" as defined by the World Health Organization.

- It is now recognized that at least 20 percent or more of all people attending any hospital clinic do not have a specific disease that can account for their symptoms; these are classified as medically unexplained symptoms, somatization, and nonorganic disorders, such as fibromyalgia, chronic regional pain syndrome, chronic low back pain, migraine and headache, irritable bowel syndrome, chronic fatigue syndrome, and myalgic encephalomyelitis. The biomedical model of illness cannot explain these illnesses at all and has no efficacious treatment. Furthermore, 5 to 10 percent of inpatient beds may be occupied by such patients.

- In conventional medicine, doctors are only concerned with the symptoms of the illness. They question the patient superficially and reject subjective symptoms. Diagnosis of the illness is based mainly on the results of the laboratory tests and imaging findings, to the point of totally ignoring emotional aspects. This approach eventually leads to identifying the person as a physical body, composed of organs, tissues, and cells in which biochemical processes occur. Conventional medicine aims mainly to treat the symptoms by using chemical medication that is identical for everyone deviating from the norm and is able to return these processes to "normal" values.

- Conventional medicine views the human body as a mechanical system (the heart is treated as a pump, the kidneys as filters, and the lungs as an oxidation organ) with disease caused by an intracellular chemical disorder, for which reason diseases are treated with chemical medications.

- Medical personnel operate according to exact guidelines developed by medical and surgical associations, which so often are suitable to the illness but not to the individual patient.

- Despite the claim that modern medicine relies on "evidence," in practice, less than 40 percent of the treatments operate on that principle.

- There is no explanation for why the rate of invalidity, as indicated by medically confirmed sickness benefit claims, is increasing while at the same time the success of medical diagnosis and treatment is improving.

- There is no reciprocal relationship between the doctor and the patient; the doctor prefers the patient to be passive, adhering closely to the treatment instructions and minimizing as far as possible all requests for explanations.

- Medicine supports aggressive intervention in treating the illness and adopts harsh and blatant terms for diverse phenomena (the "war" against cancer, to "kill" bacteria, to "eradicate" the illness, etc.) causing the patient to develop a negative attitude toward the problem from which he or she suffers and creating emotional difficulties for possible solutions.

- The main ammunition in conventional medicine is surgery, chemotherapy, radiology, and medication, which are subject to rigorous laws and rigid prescriptions based on the results of clinical research and study methods. This approach determines the schematic attitude to the patient based on standard intervention, without recognizing the uniqueness of each patient and without seeing the singular manifestation of the symptoms in him or her.

- Expanding the treatment possibilities as a result of the development of modern science and the enormous quantity of accumulated studies and information forces medicine to specialize in narrow and specific areas. From day to day, medicine discovers new damaged biochemical and genetic processes, which are described in detail, but without seeking the reason for these changes. This organic medicine overspecializes in diverse types of illnesses while losing the global and tolerant approach. This increasing process of overspecialization endangers the holistic (from the word *whole*, complete) character of medicine, which is distancing itself from the general image of the doctor and the concept of health as defined by the WHO.

- Conventional medicine is far less effective than complementary medicine in a variety of areas, such as illness prevention, preventing physical suffering without an organic disease, chronic illness, and emotional illness as well as offering a solution to the patient's emotional and spiritual needs.

- The basic problem of conventional medicine stems from being based on empirical data and research results, but without laws or principles that support these data or are based on them. One can thus conclude that medicine is based on opinions and assessment that can sometimes change in extreme ways.

- In order to solve the problems of health, conventional medicine is dependent on very expensive technological solutions that afford a tremendous social and economic burden, even when they are not always essential or effective. In its enthusiasm for technology, conventional medicine forgot the holistic facet of humankind, lost the global and patient approach, and overlooked simple and effective methods of treatment, such as dietary adjustment, relaxation training, basic breathing exercises, psychological counseling, or even spiritual counseling in order for the patient to be able to identify his or her goals in life, recognize and express his or her ambitions, satisfy his or her needs, cope with the surroundings and even alter them should it be necessary, improve his or her quality of life, and attain the happiness that will lead him or her to full physical, emotional, social, and spiritual well-being and thereby achieve health, as defined by the WHO.

- Patients want guides to help them navigate the confusing maze of therapeutic options, particularly when conventional approaches are relatively ineffective or even harmful.[3]

For all these reasons and more, numerous patients are not happy with modern medicine. Patients increasingly feel that medicine has become too commercial and that doctors are too busy to spend time with them. They rarely spend even fifteen minutes with the patient. Patients are unhappy with the impersonal nature of modern medicine, especially when the doctor spends more time looking at their lab reports, CT scans, or ultrasound or angiographic findings than listening or speaking to them. While it is true that patients need technology, they also need tender, loving care; after all, doctors need to look after not only their medical problems, but also their emotional needs![2]

Consequently, there is a feeling of disappointment among the public, which leads to the search for alternative methods and an upsurge toward alternative and complementary medicine.

Complementary Medicine and Alternative Medicine CAM

Complementary-alternative medicine is a general term that encompasses a very large array of different systems and therapies derived from a variety of ancient methods of treatment. Some of those are known and even acceptable to the medical community, while others are mostly obscure. The one thing those methods have in common is the aspect of energy. Most of them are based on the principle that there is an energy flowing steadily through the body, giving it life and vitality. A disease is an obstruction of the energy flow. Indian, Chinese, Japanese, and other Asian cultures are based on this main principle. It is important to remember that medicine is just one aspect of a given culture.

A deep examination of the various medicines related to different cultures will reveal the fact that they apply different and seemingly unrelated treatment methods. Indian medicine practitioners mainly focus on the energy centers, the chakras, while Chinese medicine is more concerned with the flow of energy along the meridians.

Homeopathy, acupuncture, shiatsu, reflexology, electro-acupuncture, magnetic healing, Bach remedies, essential oils, Reiki, and energy healing are all methods that deal with the energetic level. An improvement in the condition of the energetic level will improve physical functions and mental states. Bach flower remedies, for example, affect the state of energy that is directly related to the state of mind. These methods address the mental aspect and consider it important in the course of the treatment. Still, in most cases, alternative medicine healers will examine some mental issue that went out of balance because of a certain physical energetic disorder and failure to address the primal problem that is the cause of the energetic disturbance.

Each therapist has his or her own history, scientific assumptions, claims, and unique techniques. Some developed in the Far East, but new theories have developed in the West, most of which are based on the existence of primary energy, which provides life and vitality to living organisms. Some of the methods are intended for the broad treatment of conditions, and others concentrate on a unique or on several aspects of physical and mental health.

Alternative medicine, also known as *holistic alternative medicine* or complementary medicine, refers to every treatment of the body and the soul intended to prevent or to heal a disease. It offers a markedly different perspective through methods based on the principle of integration, which results in a balance between the body, the soul, and the psyche, and, theoretically at least, the intense connection between them. It treats the patient as a whole, hence the popular term, *holistic medicine.* Doctors practicing alternative medicine sit down and talk to the patient; they touch and feel him or her and ask many questions. Often, tender, loving care and personal attention are all that alternative medicine practitioners have to offer, but they do so extremely well indeed. There is no doubt of the efficacy of the placebo effect, and even the simple act of touching the patient can have a therapeutic benefit. Alternative medicine doctors are also very good at reassuring patients, in contrast with the coldly scientific approach of Western medicine.

The assumption in complementary medicine is that when we touch our bodies we affect the soul, and alternately, a change in the soul affects the physical condition. The main objective of holistic treatment is to strengthen natural forces of healing and balance the three components of humankind: body, soul, and psyche. Alternative medicine actually ranges from Ayurveda medicine to vitamin therapy.

Despite the development of conventional medicine and the technological progress it employs, we are witness to increasing interest in methods of treatment in complementary medicine. Thus, for example, at the end of the 1990s, 57 percent of the population in Australia used complementary medicine, as did 49 percent in France and 46 percent in Germany.

Between the years 1991 and 1997, the use of medicinal herbs increased in the United States by 380 percent and the use of vitamins by 130 percent.

A survey published in the United States of a representative sample of thirty thousand adults over the age of eighteen found that 36 percent of the adult citizens used alternative and complementary medicine.[11]

The survey provides important information on reasons that led people to avail themselves of alternative and complementary medicine:

- 55 percent of them used alternative and complementary medicine because they believed that the combination with conventional medicine could help more.
- 50 percent thought it would be interesting to try.
- 28 percent believed that conventional medicine could not help solve their problems.
- 26 percent used alternative and complementary medicine following the recommendation of someone from the medical world.
- 13 percent of those who used alternative and complementary medicine felt that conventional medicine was too expensive.

Recent years show clear evidence of an increase in the use of complementary medicine, manifested in several clinics that are directly connected with hospitals, the opening of departments of complementary medicine within the hospital, the addition of courses of study in medical schools, and complementary treatments offered by the sick funds.[12]

Alternative medicine is actually based on four major values:

- choosing a natural medication over a synthetic drug
- examining the root of the problem, not just treating the symptom
- viewing the individual as a single entity, instead of going after the diseases
- focusing on preventive medicine instead of fighting diseases after their outbreak

The demand for solutions offered by complementary medicine is increasing, and most hospitals now allow alternative treatments should conventional medicine fail to help or should the patient prefer this. Several explanations are proposed for the increasing interest in complementary medicine:

- It offers a better solution to chronic diseases, for example, but homeopathy was also found to be effective in providing first aid.
- Most complementary medicine methods attempt to treat the original cause of the illness and consider, rather than ignore, the symptoms.
- Alternative medication focuses mainly on prevention, relates to the person individually, and relies on the holistic approach, which views the patient as one entity comprising body, soul, and psyche.
- Holistic medicine allows gentle and long-term intervention to enable the body's healing forces to create a situation of recovery using natural medication that has withstood the test of hundreds, and sometimes thousands, of years
- Complementary medicine practitioners adapt the method of treatment to the patient and are not bound by a rigid scientific

book of rules. Thus the treatment is also subjective and is not uniform for all patients

- Since most of the alternative medicine practitioners are not subject to instructions or to fixed codes, they can totally devote themselves to the patient.
- Research shows that the consultation process and holistic approach adopted by practitioners of complementary medicine make patients feel more in control of their illness.[13]

The Disadvantages of Alternative Medicine

The practice of alternative medicine in India today offers us a good example of the situation of alternative medicine in general. Such medicine does not have a universally accepted scientific basis; hence, it is difficult to rigorously analyze its claims. Since there is no need for formal publication or peer review in alternative systems of medicine, there is little scientific documentation available on their efficacy or side effects, and it becomes difficult to confirm claims or dispute them. Consequently, one has to blindly trust the doctor. Authoritative journals or texts are difficult to find, and most publications use little scientific rigor, being based mostly on anecdotal case reports with little documentation or proof. Moreover, since there is no official monitoring of the practitioners of alternative medicine, anyone can claim success and get away with it. Moreover, since there are few formal training requirements, anyone can practice alternative medicine with minimal skills or qualifications.

The increasing use of alternative methods is also accompanied by a rise in reports of side effects and possible damage, mainly since they are unsupervised. In China, there is extensive use of medicinal plants and natural methods as part of the culture in parallel to conventional medicine. However, between the years 1990 and 1999, four thousand cases of side effects were reported due to the use of traditional Chinese medicine, and in 2000, 9,854 cases of complications connected to these treatments were reported. Many of the alternative products are sold outside China. A survey of 142 countries for the WHO found that these products can be sold without a medical prescription in ninety-nine countries; in thirty-nine countries, traditional products were in use for independent treatment and were sold or prepared by friends or by the sick person him- or herself. This tendency raised concern regarding the quality of the products, their medical contribution, and the lack of tracking.

Therefore, WHO came out with instructions intended for the government, the health systems, and patients in 2004 that endeavored to provide the user with available information, a channel for reporting harmful medicinal reactions, and a way to track practitioners and define essential skills for treatment. WHO also encouraged reciprocal relations between complementary and alternative medicine and biomedicine, standardization of approaches to treatment, and coordination between the different medical approaches, educating the patient to insist on a report of the practitioner's skills and on the essence of the treatment and its relevance to the medical problem, examining prices and clarifying possible side effects.[14]

So we can aver that alternative medicine is not immune to disadvantages. In fact, many opponents of complementary medicine raise the following claims:

- Despite the global spread of complementary medicine, most of its methods were not assessed using accepted scientific tools and controlled experiments.
- Due to the difference in the basic approach between the two methods, modern medical practitioners believe that most alternative methods are based on theories that lack any scientific basis.
- Alternative medicine can cause damage by neglecting conventional methods of treatment, especially as regards a serious or mechanical problem, with which conventional medicine can help more in preventing decline in the patient's

condition and even in saving his or her life, such as in a situation of new constriction symptoms or myocardial infarction.

- There is an accumulation of evidence of considerable damage due to alternative treatment.

- Health shops and pharmacies are swamped with products whose quality, effectiveness, and safety of use are not known.

- The lack of suitable training of alternative medicine practitioners and the lack of supervision of them are liable to result in the involvement of untrained therapists in treatment that is liable to endanger life.

- Despite the claim that these are holistic methods, close observation of the various methods indicates that there is no connection between them and the practitioners focus on one aspect, such as reflexology, iridology, acupuncture, or osteopathy. A therapist specializing in one method is not necessarily familiar with another method. This returns us to the problem of specialization and underspecialization existing in conventional medicine. Thus some of the methods of alternative healing overlap, while others have nothing in common.

Both conventional and alternative medicine set for themselves the objective of not causing damage to the patient, but it would seem that this objective is no longer so clear and distinct among conventional health institutions. In Australia, for example, hospitals are ranked third as the main cause of death.[4-5]

In the United States, infections that are transferred through blood products in the hospital framework cause 62,000 cases of death annually, and the mortality rate there, as a result of surgical intervention, is 25,000 per annum.[6]

In American hospitals, more than one million people annually have been severely hurt and 2.5 million patients a year develop side effects to medication, resulting in 100,000 deaths.[7]

Hence complications connected to American hospitals rank fifth in the causes of death, after cancer, heart disease, accidents, and cerebral hemorrhage.[8]

Conventional medicine maintains the close trinity—medicine-medication-the pharmaceutical industry. Heading the order of priorities of the pharmaceutical industry is the goal of making a profit, in contrast to the objective of most conventional doctors, whose order of priorities is still headed by the patient's health and welfare.

However, the complex reciprocal relations between medicine and the pharmaceutical industry blur the scientific norms in favor of bureaucratic laws; the impossible task of facing the pressures and timetables and also the fear of mistakes and of "medical negligence" distance the conventional doctor from his or her primary goal and make him or her, even if unconsciously, a marketing tool for the pharmaceutical industry.

One of the claims against complementary medicine is that it does not meet the scientific criteria, that scientific research has not proved its effectiveness. One of the reasons for this is that most sources of funding for medical research come from national organizations and pharmaceutical industries, which are not enthusiastic about supporting research that will prove the effectiveness of changes in lifestyle or of vitamins and other natural products. Thus a minuscule proportion of the research budgets is allocated to holistic medical research. Furthermore, in most academic institutions, there is no suitable infrastructure for complementary medical research, and most practitioners of complementary medicine are not doctors or connected to medical institutions that enable them to be involved in research.

Moreover, conventional medicine usually opposes treatment using natural means even after their effectiveness has been proven scientifically. (Germany is an exception in this respect.) Nevertheless, one can distinguish an increasing number of doctors and researchers who turn to natural remedies and publish their work in traditional professional papers. Thus, for example, the advantages of antioxidants were published at length by researchers from the Harvard University School of Medicine and by researchers at other famous institutions. Other materials, such as folic acid and vitamin B, were studied in university laboratories and were found to be effective in preventing or improving cases of heart attack, cerebral hemorrhage, occasional limping, atherosclerosis, kidney disease, cancer of the large intestine, loss of hearing, and Alzheimer's.[9]

Thus for example, in Germany, *Ginkgo biloba* is the most frequently prescribed natural medicine that has proven effectiveness in preventing and treating Alzheimer's. Another natural medication known as *Serenoa repens* is prescribed in Germany in 90 percent of the cases of prostate cancer, while in the United States, three hundred thousand surgical operations are preformed to solve this problem. There is no doubt that these afford an important economic source for surgeons and for companies manufacturing equipment and pharmaceuticals, but they are more dangerous and less pleasant for the patients.[10]

The helplessness of conventional medicine in treating chronic disease, manifested in methods of treatment intended to conceal the symptoms instead of healing the disease, aroused the concern that the human race is in danger of losing its health and caused a rush to obtain advice and treatment from complementary medicine practitioners.

Integrative Medicine

A healthy person has hope, and someone who has hope
has everything.

—Arab proverb

Integrated medicine is practicing medicine in a way that selectively
incorporates elements of complementary and alternative medicine into
comprehensive treatment plans alongside solidly orthodox methods of
diagnosis and treatment.

Integration, or combination, of methods of treatment is a real need first
manifested in recent years in the medical literature. However, less than
a decade ago, complementary medicine was rejected by conventional
doctors, and in academic circles, it was considered to be marginal
medicine. Today, complementary medicine attracts the mainstream in
academia as well.[15]

In recent years, we clearly saw that the patients' attitudes toward their
own diseases has been changing and Western medicine can no longer
ignore the fact that half of their current patients receive treatment
from complementary medicine practitioners. People seek alternative
ways to solve health issues that were not resolved through conventional
methods. In the United States alone, the number of people seeking
help from alternative medicine practitioners went up from 427 million
in 1990 to 629 million in 1997, a year in which some 42 percent of
the US population received treatment by at least one complementary

medicine practitioner.[16] Use of alternative medicine is becoming more popular in industrialized countries. Studies conducted worldwide show that more than 10 percent of the residents of Denmark applied alternative medicine, while in Australia, their number has reached 49 percent.

Many hospitals and clinics recently opened departments for nonconventional medicine, and certain health insurance companies already pay for treatment by acupuncture, homeopathy, reflexology, and more. Western medicine as a whole has started paying more attention to the mental aspects, but this is still done in a general and unfocused fashion. Alternative medicine is gaining popularity and is approached more, mainly because people are dissatisfied with conventional medicine, and primarily with its failure to address the humane aspects of disease.

The Federation of State Medical Boards of the United States developed *Model Guidelines for the Use of Complementary and Alternative Therapies in Medical Practice.* The guidelines focus on "encouraging the medical community to adopt consistent standards, ensuring the public health and safety by facilitating the proper and effective use of both conventional and CAM treatments, while educating physicians on the adequate safeguards needed to assure these services are provided within the bounds of acceptable professional practice."[17]

According to the Consortium of Academic Health Centers for Integrative Medicine, a collaborative alliance of forty-six academic health centers dedicated to the advancement of integrative health care, "integrative medicine is the practice of medicine that reaffirms the importance of the relationship between practitioner and patient, focuses on the whole person, is informed by evidence, and makes use of all appropriate therapeutic approaches, healthcare professionals and disciplines to achieve optimal health and healing."

However, integrative medicine is the use of complementary and alternative medicine besides conventional medicine. National health institutions in the United States opened special departments in the 1990s, known as the National Center for Complementary and Alternative Medicine (NCCAM), to study complementary medicine. The goal was to explore alternative therapeutic methods in scientific terms, to train researchers in complementary medicine, and to disseminate authoritative information to the public and to professionals.

Papers published in past years show that 64 percent of American medical schools teach complementary medicine.[18] But there are large differences in content and demand for these programs, emphasizing the need for uniform and consistent curricula in order to prepare the next generation of doctors who will provide integrated medicine.

Clearly, elective courses are not sufficient to train a doctor to advise patients on complementary treatment, and therefore, the report published on behalf of the American Association of Medical Schools calls on doctors to be aware to the same extent of diverse methods of treatment using both conventional and complementary medicine.[19]

Patients nowadays are not satisfied with only conventional medicine and at the same time seek other solutions. When the patient feels comfortable involving the attending doctor and consulting him or her about complementary treatments, he or she can reconsider treatment possibilities offered to him or her. Medical research published in the *Journal of Clinical Oncology* in 2001 observes that 60 to 80 percent of cancer patients use alternative medical methods during the illness.

In the large leading medical centers in the world for treating cancer, such as in MD Anderson in Houston, Texas and the Sloan Kettering Hospital in New York, and in other important medical centers, the integration of conventional medicine and alternative-complementary medicine was found to improve the results of treatment. They thus established units for complementary-alternative medicine as part of the treatment offered there.

Real integrative treatment causes the patient to take responsibility for both prevention and for the treatment itself. Contempt and even rejection by the conventional doctor when the patient asks to use complementary medicine causes the latter to conceal the complementary treatment from him or her. Hence research shows that less than 40 percent of those using complementary medicine inform their doctors.[20-21]

The patient's need for complementary medicine should be understood by the attending doctor, if he or she wants to participate in the patient's healing process. The doctor can thereby avoid conflict with the patient's beliefs, demonstrate understandable concern of the side effects or even damage that can be caused from a particular treatment, and be able to place emphasis on the meaning and understand the message behind the illness, instead of proving the effectiveness of a particular treatment.[22-23]

The lack of communication between the patient and doctor can expose the patient to serious risks when he or she uses medicinal plants, food additives, or "natural" medication.

There is no doubt that medical training must alter the medical approach according to social needs and expectations. The integration of diverse types of medicine is a real necessity. This is the reason why many medical schools are trying to add elective courses on complementary medicine. It is interesting that this percentage has not changed since 1998, although the number of courses on complementary medicine doubled, from thirty-four in 1996 to seventy-five in 1998.[24]

It is well accepted that the time is ripe to integrate diverse modalities, such as massage, Reiki, yoga, Ayurveda, acupressure, acupuncture, hypnosis, homeopathy, naturopathy, and many others as part of a unified team rather than as competition. According to this model, a good doctor will be able to guide the patient to be aware of the strengths and limitations of each approach. The patient should feel free to explore all possible options, which should be seen to be complementary to each other. After all, the goal of all of them is to help the patient to achieve a state of complete wellness.

This kind of integration, trying to combine the best of both worlds—advanced technology with human touch, tender loving care, and personal attention—is called integrative medicine.

We see a tendency toward this track in integrative medicine. There are two dominant models of integrative medicine that have been developed. One is the selective combination of biomedical evidence and experience-based evidence of both CAM and conventional medicine. The other is the selective incorporation of exclusively evidence-based CAMs into conventional medicine. The two model types signify different levels of equity between CAM and conventional medicine, concerning the power, autonomy, and control held by each. However, we need a health-care model that will unify the two tendencies into one system that aspires to be patient-centered and holistic, with the focus on health rather than disease, prevention rather than cure, and healing rather than treatment. However, we are not satisfied with this kind of integration based on adding CAM when needed. We need one model with a new paradigm that views patients as whole humans with a physical body, a psyche, and a soul and includes these dimensions in diagnosis and treatment.

In order to combine the diverse types of medicine into unified integrative medicine, we must find a model that combines Western science with its modes of thought and intellectual experience with the intuitive human experience of the East. Once found, medicine would be one unified integrative medicine.

In order to unify the two models into one holistic model, we need to explore the basis of the two models and find a scientific model of unification.

The Encounter between the Two Worlds

The difficulty in merging the worlds of conventional and complementary medicine resides mainly in the difference in the conceptual basis on which each method is founded. These two medical approaches are differentiated by their philosophies, their understanding of life, their perception of the concept of health and the patient, and their methods of diagnosis and treatment. Conventional medicine researches and treats only that which is logical, rational, and quantifiable. In most cases, it relies on objective data and negates subjective aspects, dealing mainly with symptoms. In contrast, complementary medicine observes, researches, diagnoses, and treats also that which is not logical or rational and cannot be measured. These two medical approaches would seem to be so different that they cannot be bridged. We are thus in need of a philosophical and physical model able to combine the two approaches into the one whole unified system, enabling us to exploit the positives and the successes and avoid the negative aspects and the lack of success in each approach.

The attempt to integrate complementary and conventional medicine encounters the basic conceptual difference that seems to be impossible to bridge: while conventional medicine is based on the materialist principle; complementary medicine is based on the vitalism principle.

Materialism

The philosophy of *materialism* holds that the only thing that can be truly proven to exist is matter. The world as composed of matter and space and changes as the result of combinations or movements of atoms. All things are composed of material, and all phenomena (including consciousness) are the result of material interactions; therefore, matter is the only substance.

In the eighteenth century, philosophers turned to materialism hoping that it would increase knowledge of the physical world and of humankind. They believed that the properties of living beings arose from the complexity of their organization and rejected sharp distinctions between the living and the nonliving. Nineteenth-century materialists, like Hermann von Helmholtz, Ludwig Büchner, and Jacob Moleschott, attempted to confute the prominence vitalism enjoyed in medicine. Their studies suggested to them that what had been explained as vital forces could be better understood as purely physical (that is, material) phenomena. The nervous system, for instance, could adequately explain mental activities like reason, memory, or the emotions, behaviors vitalists were inclined to associate with the soul or life forces.

The basic principle of scientific materialism avers that:

- There are only physical objects, and there is nothing beyond. The approach is based on observation of a world that functions in a deterministic, causal manner.

- It is possible to understand and explain everything based on primary physical laws. Everything, including ourselves and everything that is alive, is controlled by physical laws that are the sole laws that direct our ambitions, hopes, and desires.
- The external and the objective realities are primary, and everything, including intellectual phenomena, emanates from it or is a result of this reality.
- Life depends absolutely on physiological processes, and they are perceived as a chain of chemical reactions in a watery solution within the cell, causing the appearance of an electronic field (psyche) that regulates other processes characterizing the living cell. Thus psyche is secondary to the chemical activity of body cells and disappears when certain processes cease functioning.
- "I am the body," and therefore the body is the main entity in our lives. We are guided by its material demands to the point that it plans our future or revives our past.
- According to this approach, life starts at birth and concludes with death. Its main purpose focuses on reorganizing or exchanging material goods (including the body) in order to create maximum material satisfaction and pleasure. We must focus all our energies in this direction, since we cannot have any other objective.
- The well-being of our bodies is our primary concern; thus the body makes us its servant and prisoner, and we must meet its existential demands, such as territory, food and drink, and sex and reproduction, and protect it from internal threat, such as pain and sickness, or external threats to sources of subsistence— the home, income, survival, children, or weather conditions.
- According to this philosophy, the soul is explained as a physical and biological phenomenon secondary to the body.
- This approach does not believe in the existence of the spiritual aspect, and the parapsychological phenomena are an illusion or can be explained by physical laws.

This materialistic approach led to technological progress and human development, but basic disadvantages exist in understanding life, and it is incapable of solving the psychophysical problem. A perception, according to which only the body exists, does not facilitate freedom, since everything is physical and causal and the laws of nature control everything. The emotional causes that motivate us to act are external and stem from the residue of the past (childhood trauma, paternal attitude toward the child at a young age, etc.). The fact that we are part of a causal chain establishes determinism and therefore does not provide us with the possibility to choose.

According to this approach, the body affects the psyche. It affects the psyche to create awareness, but the spirit itself has no physical impact. Thus the spirit cannot be independent since the spiritual phenomena are the result of the chemical reactions in the physical body; hence, it is subordinate to the body. But how can material be aware or relate to something? And how can something emotional create a physical phenomenon? And how can thoughts generate activities? The objective scientific perception cannot explain the subjective point of view existing in each of us.

The Vitalistic Approach

Vitalism is a doctrine holding that living organisms are fundamentally different from nonliving entities because they contain a vital principle, some nonphysical element distinct from physicochemical forces. Vitalism has a long history in medical philosophies. Most traditional healing practices posited that disease was the result of some imbalance in the vital energies that distinguish living from nonliving matter. In the Western tradition, founded by Hippocrates, these vital forces were associated with the four temperaments and humors; Eastern traditions posited similar forces, such as qi and prana.

Vitalism became prominent among physicians in the late seventeenth and early eighteenth centuries. They emphasized the soul as the critical determinant of human physiology and function, although they had different responses to questions of the specific, nonmechanical entity of life, its effects, and its connection to the body in terms of cause and effect.

Late nineteenth- and early twentieth-century vitalists, like Hans Driesch and Henri Louis Bergson, insisted that a mechanism could not adequately explain the development of the embryo or the spiritual dimension of human life and the vital energy of the mind. Insofar as there is a contemporary immaterialist position, it focuses specifically on functions of mind rather than on life in general.

In contrast to the materialistic approach, the vitalistic approach asserts that:

- A primary energy exists that controls the entire universe (God, universal energy, the global psyche).
- The processes of life cannot be explained by the laws of physics and chemistry alone; life is in some part self-determining.
- The presence of this energy differentiates between animate and inanimate material and affords it attributes of life.
- Life depends absolutely on the presence of a life spark or energy, which is termed differently in different cultures: Chi (in China), Ki (in Japan), Parna (India), Orgone (by Wilhelm Reich), or the bioenergetic field and animal magnetism (Mesmer), which some equate with the soul.
- Humans are soul and are only spiritual. The psyche is the functional part of the soul. The spirit has no time or place and does not belong to the world of matter. Since this is the case, the rules of physics do not apply to it.
- The spirit is defined as being distinct from the body and survives the death of the body. The soul thought to confer the inner awareness of each living being and to be the true basis for consciousness.
- Health is a condition in which life energies are balanced and flow without blockages.
- The essence of life is spiritual, and illness is secondary to a lack of balance of life energies, where sickness also originates. There is something superior that sets the illness into motion before it materializes in corporal pathology, in laboratory tests, and in structural changes.
- Life does not start with birth and does not conclude with death, but they are a transition between various reincarnations in order to benefit the souls and to return to the Creator pure and clean of all sin.

- The soul is the center of life, and therefore, the body is of secondary importance; sometimes, torment of the body leads to purity of the soul.
- Life is a developing process directed by consciousness. It cannot be explained completely, only through understanding the chemical processes that occur within the cell.
- Development and integration are trends that operate in a person and cannot be constructed on the foundation of mechanical causal perception.

Nonetheless, there is a third model of consciousness which is romanticism. This is a movement stressing strong emotion as a source of aesthetic experience, placing emphasis on such emotions, especially those that are experienced in confronting the sublimity of untamed nature. It argues for a "natural" epistemology of human activities as conditioned by nature in the form of language, custom, and usage.

Is there a way to fuse these three basic approaches?

Unifying Forces

The vitalism model is based on the idea that mysterious intelligent energy exists, and the known laws of physics do not apply to it. But the truth is that a mysterious force also exists that causes the heart to beat, hair to grow, and food to be digested. That same force enables one to read this book and to process the information read at this moment. Many philosophers saw reality as motivated by spiritual entities. Diverse streams in psychology adopted this approach, recognizing that the psyche cannot be understood only on the basis of instinctive drives and events from the past, as other streams in psychology try to explain it.

Our choice is an integration of philosophy and physics, mathematics and theology, technology and arts. Therefore, for us to deal with integrative medicine, we must clarify the philosophy of physics, recognize the physics of philosophy, and develop the art of technology.

Before we combine different methods of medicine, we must understand better the structure of the human physical body, the nature of the soul, the function of the psyche, and the interaction between them. To understand the characteristics of these components and their attributes, we must return to our origin, to nature. Understanding the basic laws that guide the universe may help us to clarify the nature of the different components of the human being. This allows us to integrate and apply the existing knowledge in one clear model. This integrated model should help us ultimately to understand the origin of the differences in treatment in the diverse methods and the principles upon which they are based. We will discover that the different disciplines are meant to attain normality and harmony in one or more components of the human being. Conventional medicine intends mainly to treat the physical body, while psychology deals with the psyche. Different methods of the alternative complementary medicine try to attain harmony between the diverse components of the human body, psyche, and soul and the environment.

Holism Unifies the Materialism with Vitalism

Both approaches, materialism and vitalism, are correct; each one describes a part of the reality, and these two models divide the Western material and mechanistic model from the Eastern energy-oriented model. Conventional medicine is based on the mechanistic model, and Eastern alternative and complementary medicines are based on the vitalistic one. It becomes obvious that conventional medicine based on chemistry and physics is not enough to solve the riddle or explain the full complexity of the physiology of the human body. It is only when we add the energetic dimension to chemistry and physics that we understand the full expression of human life in every dimension to include the spiritual dimension, which is completely neglected in modern medicine. This spiritual essence does not intend to override scientific laws but rather expands our point of view to include very high-frequency physical reality.

These two concepts can be explained using modern physical terms. In classical physics, everything in the universe is made of either matter or energy. What makes matter special is mass; you can weigh it—something you can't do with light.

Modern physics reduced matter down to atoms, then to protons, neutrons, and electrons, and then again to quarks, leptons, and other oddly named particles. Albert Einstein entered the scene with his famous theories of relativity, and these tiny particles suddenly looked much different from classical physics' black-and-white division of matter and energy.

Einstein's theories led to the famous equation, $E = mc^2$, which says that energy and mass are actually two different forms of the same thing. Mass and matter might better be looked at as a form of very dense energy. In fact, mass can be converted to energy and vice versa. Mass can be expressed as a particle or as a mass. (In my book, *The Seven Universal Principles and the Seventh Sense*, I describe elemental particles, such as electrons, quarks, and photons as vortices. These vortices were created during the big bang from the primordial vacuum energy field.)

This is the wave-particle duality that represents the two concepts, materialism and vitalism. Both are connected by the vacuum energy that exists in space even in the absence of matter. The holistic model connects these two approaches, the natural systems (physical, biological, chemical, social, economic, mental, linguistic, etc.) and their properties are viewed as wholes, not as collections of parts. This often includes the view that systems somehow function as wholes and that their functioning cannot be fully understood solely in terms of their component parts.[25-26]

Reductionism may be viewed as the complement of holism. Reductionism analyzes a complex system by subdividing or *reducing* it to more fundamental parts. For example, the processes of biology are reducible to chemistry, and the laws of chemistry are explained by physics.

The Holistic Model in Medicine

The perception of medicine undergoes an important change when the two different approaches pertaining to health and sickness—the biomedical or scientific approach and the holistic experiential approach—are combined. The former reduces the illness to a disturbance in the biochemical process in cells and tissues and relies mainly on the therapeutic model that is intended to restore the biochemical processes to normal, while holistic medicine relies on the healing model, which emphasizes the mutual action and reaction between diverse factors—biochemical, environmental, emotional, and spiritual.

Our eventual goal as doctors, psychologists, and healers is to create one medicine able to maintain health by achieving physical, emotional, spiritual, and social well-being and place its main emphasis on prevention. Conventional medicine and complementary medicine are like two sides of the same coin, two poles of one system, in which each complements the other to form a complete whole. The holistic model describes and analyzes the relationships between body, psyche, and soul in order to obtain the complete state of well-being.

Throughout history, it has been recognized that the human mind is capable of three kinds of knowledge or three modes of consciousness, which have often been termed the *rational, emotional,* and *intuitive* and have traditionally been associated with science, religion, and art. Western medicine is based upon mechanistic principles, rational knowledge, and empiricism acquired through scientific research and empirical experimental evidence. This knowledge is derived from the experiences we have had with objectives and events in our everyday environment. It belongs to the realm of the intellect, whose function is to discriminate, divide, compare, measure, and categorize.

Complementary and alternative medicine, on the other hand, is founded on the vitalism principle and mostly on Eastern mysticism, which is based on direct insights into the nature of reality. This is the intuitive type of knowledge that is often devalued in favor of rational, scientific knowledge. Rational knowledge, however, would be useless if not complemented by the intuition, which gives scientists new insights and makes them creative. Conventional medicine provides the material needs of the body, and complementary medicine provides the tools for psychological satisfaction and spiritual fulfillment.

The need to combine Western physics (science) with philosophical thought and the intellectual experience of the Western world with the intuitive human experience of the East is therefore clear.

Medicine cannot but appear as one unified integrative medicine that relates to people as entities comprising body, soul, and psyche. Consequently, this medicine will manage to integrate the most modern treatments based on physics, mathematics, technology, and statistics, which take into consideration mainly the physical body, with healing methods derived from ancient philosophies that consider the emotional and spiritual aspects of humankind and have survived the test of time and proved their effectiveness and reliability, and create a new unified integrative medicine.

This kind of medicine has far broader significance and purpose than medicine today. It is able to combine the best of Western scientific medicine with a broader understanding of the nature of illness, healing, and wellness. It focuses mainly on health and prevention and not only on the illness and treatment. Easily integrated by all medical specialties and professional areas and by all health systems, its use not only improves patient care; it also improves the cost-effectiveness of health-care delivery providers and payers.

Unified integrative medicine sees the patient as an integration of body, soul, and psyche, emphasizing and caring for all the factors that can affect the quality of life in order to achieve physical, psychological, social, and spiritual well-being. It therefore considers the body integrity by regulating diet, physical activity, breathing, sexual behavior, quality of rest and sleep, and the type of relationships with others. It emphasizes love, connections, and support for others to achieve hope, comfort, and inner peace. Integrative medicine should enable us to examine the quality of an individual's inner resources, the ability to give and receive spiritual love, and the types of relationships and connections that exist with the self, the community, the environment, and nature.

Our mission is to help the patient to expand his or her current state of consciousness, to be aware of his or her needs, to search for meaning and purpose, to achieve greater creativity and the elevation of the mind, and to increase compassion and unconditional love in order to afford a feeling of release, satisfaction, personal fulfillment, wholeness, and happiness, and as a result, well-being and health.

Thus, eventually, when we enter the treatment room, we must exercise sagacity rather than applying the method of treatment. We have to develop our ability to listen, patience, awareness of the purity of our intentions, and love of what we are doing.

However, before we define illness and disease, we need to redefine life and health, taking into consideration the relationship between the three components of the human being.

What Model We Propose

This is an era in which we are exposed to enormous amounts of constantly flowing information. New technologies, mainly the Internet, allow not only the communication of information from and to the various medical systems but also the merger of old and new data as well a new understanding of natural phenomena that were so far considered mystical knowledge or even lost in the darkness of the occult. The search for a theory to understand human nature better, led me to look for a holistic model that integrated all aspects of our lives into one model. This could not be done without the search for a universal theory that could be applied in all aspects from physics through biology to spirituality. I found that with seven principles, we can describe everything from the quantum and spiritual realm to the material world.

From this, integrative theory was born.

Medicine is whatever is able to restore and maintain health. The right of a person to health services is one of the basic rights in most developed countries. But what is "health"? The World Health Organization (WHO) defined the general perception of health in the Introduction to the Constitution of the World Health Organization (1948) thus: "Health is a state of complete physical, mental and social wellbeing and not merely the absence of disease or infirmity."

It further states, "Health promotion is the process of enabling people to increase control over, and to improve, their health ... To reach a state of complete physical, mental and social well-being, an individual or group must be able to identify and to realize aspirations, to satisfy needs, and to change or cope with the environment" (Ottawa Charter for Health Promotion, 1986).

These definitions are our starting points and are oriented to obtain and maintain a state of well-being through the realization of aspirations, satisfying needs, and coping with environmental difficulties.

The holistic view of well-being and quality of life is not only associated with a balance between the physical and the psychological bodies; it must also include aspects of the spirit—the soul. The human being is made of three main components: body, psyche, and soul.

Energy is being absorbed from food and air through the skin and the energy centers, the chakras. That energy is distributed throughout the body—through blood, other bodily liquids, and the meridians—all the way to the aura around the individual cells and the entire body. Denying the fact that the spirit gives life to the physical body, moves it on, and makes it flow means losing the main thing—the uniqueness of the human essence.

An understanding of the qualities of the vital energy is the basis for an understanding of physiological processes; thus, we understand that the body is practically the physical expression of the soul (the energy body). Thoughts and emotions are also energy whose source is the same life energy within the body. Blocking our emotions or using them to exhaustion will affect the body's life energy, and the way we express our emotions and deal with crises in our lives will determine whether we keep flowing and being happy or stop the life energy in one of the four stages of life.

The method suggested in this book is unique in the way it clearly and fully defines the linkage between a given mental crisis and the specific affected organ, while associating between the mode of reaction and the specific type of illness that appears in the relevant limb. Thus, by observing the disease, we can understand the nature of the crisis and identify the appropriate reaction type needed for its treatment.

Identifying the crisis is the first important step in the healing process. With the help of the seventh sense, which each of us can develop, we can not only identify the mental crisis underlying the physical ailment but also its source and the year in which it occurred. At the same time, this type of diagnosis creates a deep spiritual connection between the patient and healer. This new view is very important when we try to understand the internal workings of the human body or the functioning of the brain. Here, for the first time, we gain a better understanding of cerebral processes; hence, we can understand the association between the structure of the nervous system and the expressions of our consciousness.

Viewing a disease as the result of unbalanced energy, which follows from a mental crisis that was not properly processed, will necessarily lead to changing the definition of illness. Even before an energetic blockage emerges as a physical disease, it has already caused functional disorders on the mental and physical levels. At this stage, when the patient seeks help from the medical establishment—where he or she undergoes an inspection process that includes blood tests, X-ray images, or other medical examinations that fail to find the reasons for his or her grievances—the patient might feel frustrated, fearing that the physician and the medical establishment do not understand him or her or even doubt his or her complaints. In any event, because it might take a long time, sometimes many years before an energy block emerges as a physical disease, it is hard to associate between the mental crisis and the subsequent disease. Locating the energetic disorder in the interim stage—after the energy block appeared and before the disease shows up—is critical because the patient can be treated then by simple and painless means. It will help the patient understand the mental reason for the energy block. The conventional definition of a disease, therefore, is based on findings that emerge from physical alterations or subjective symptoms. However, the physical symptoms appear at almost the last stage in a chain of mental and energetic changes.

A person who suffers no pain and shows no symptoms is in a neutral state, but this is not enough. There is no suffering in this state, but there is no joy either. This is the middle ground from which we can ascend to meet our happiness or descend to misery and disease. The road to happiness goes through attention, well-processed crises, and offering love. These three will lead us to spiritual growth and a sense of satisfaction that is based on the recognition that we are fulfilling our destiny in this lifetime. Conversely, improperly processed mental crises create energy blocks that lead to dissatisfaction, mental suffering, physical symptoms, functional impairment, frustration, declining vitality levels, accelerated aging, and death. We must redefine the purpose of life and the goal of medicine. We need to aspire to a higher quality of life, while redefining health, functional disorder, and disease.

It is a basic truth that the conventional medical systems often face serious economic difficulties and thus simply cannot "afford" to give each patient enough time and attention. To overcome this problem, physicians tend to focus on the physical symptoms of the disease, trying to resolve them as quickly as possible. As a result, specialized physicians address each specific symptom of a disease. Should other symptoms appear that do not fall within his or her area of knowledge, the specialist will not address them and refer the patient to another specialist. For example, a person suffering from asthma will see a lung specialist. At the same time, he or she might complain about psoriasis and an inflammation in the back and the elbow. The lung specialist will find no relation whatsoever between the asthma and the other symptoms and, at best, will send his or her patient to an orthopedist to look at the elbow while a dermatologist will be asked to examine the psoriasis. In the holistic approach, asthma is a symptom of fear of abandonment that was not elaborated or fully expressed on the emotional level. This creates tension on the bronchial level, which, coupled with additional external and emotional stimuli, causes asthma. On the energetic level, there is a clear connection between the skin and the lungs. Excess tension in the lungs will lead to tension in the skin. As a result, psoriasis will appear on the skin in areas that are tense for other reasons, such as mechanical tension in the joint area. Chinese medicine tells us that the lung meridian crosses the arm muscle that is connected to the tendon going to the thumb. Tension in the lungs will create tension along the lung meridian and, as a result, excessive tension will appear in the muscle it runs through. Ongoing tension might lead to small lacerations and miniruptures in the muscle tissue, which will result in pain and inflammation.

As we can see, our patient is actually suffering from a single medical problem that is simply expressed on several levels. The real problem is the original fear of abandonment by one or both parents that was not processed. The side that is involved with the elbow pain and psoriasis will clarify if it is related to the father, the right side, or the mother, the left side. This is what the healer should be addressing until the energy block is released; then the bronchioles will relax so there is no more asthma and the psoriasis and elbow pain will disappear.

Chinese medicine addresses the energy blockages in meridians and tries to renew the flow through acupuncture, digito-pressure, moxa, etc. However, these do not address or resolve the real cause of these blockages, which are stress and psychological conflicts. Furthermore, traditional Chinese medicine addresses specific emotional aspects related to meridians and related organs. However, it describes the emotional aspect related to the specific organ and meridian as a result of energy depletion. In our method, special attention is given to the real cause of the blockage and not the emotional and mental aspect as the result of the blockage. For example, according to traditional Chinese medicine sadness is related to lungs; however, sadness is the result of energy depletion in the lungs and not the cause of blockage of the meridian of lungs. Traditional Indian medicine takes into consideration the blockages in chakras. Many disciplines address these blockages and try to release them by prana healing, massage, Reiki, etc. However, no one address the real cause that blocked these chakras. This book clearly and specifically describes a different course of disease, claiming that the energy block itself is a result of a mental crisis. This crisis blocks the energy in a specific chakra, which affects organs associated with the specific emotional aspect of that chakra. The energy block, due to psychological conflict, leads to physical and mental symptoms and ultimately to organic dysfunction and disease.

This approach is clearly different from the conventional medicine approach. A disease, for which we are personally responsible, is a result of a crisis that serves as a test whose aim is to expand our experience and help us take yet another step on the road to our spiritual destiny. The healing process is, therefore, a developmental process that takes one from an agonizing mental hindrance to spiritual release and gives satisfaction and a sense of profound joy.

According to this model, the future physician will play an important role in changing the way diseases are viewed and defined. Total health will be expressed through total balance between the three major components of human essence: mind, body, and soul. Maintaining a pure soul, patience, and love will be the guideline of the future physician.

The Research Method

Biomedical research is the basic research conducted to aid the body of knowledge in the field of medicine. Medical research can be divided into two general categories: the evaluation of new treatments for both safety and efficacy in what are termed clinical trials and all other research that contributes to the development of new treatments. The latter is termed *preclinical research* if its goal is specifically to elaborate knowledge for the development of new therapeutic strategies. A clinical trial is a comparison test of a medication or other medical treatment versus a placebo, other medication and devices, or the standard medical treatment for a patient's condition. Experimenters typically use placebos as a control group to compare with the test group in which patients receive the therapy being tested. It can then be determined whether results from the test group exceed the others because of the placebo effect. If they do, the therapy or pill given to the test group is assumed to have had an effect.

It is important, however, to note that the research approach to assessing CAM cannot be the same approach used in conventional medicine. Effective applied clinical research will require strong collaboration between CAM clinicians and medical researchers, reflected in research teams on grant applications. In the long run, this will also help the emergence of CAM practitioner researchers.[27]

Specific methodological difficulties in performing CAM research need to be recognized; many CAM trials have been criticized as methodologically weak. These difficulties are a key part of the CAM methodology.

- CAM practices, including acupuncture and chiropractic care, often involve significant interaction between patient and practitioner. Research within these practices has been plagued with the difficulty of creating a suitable placebo.
- CAM treatments are often individually tailored to the patient and are based on a different diagnostic process from Western medicine.
- Intervention is often complex, such as the combination of acupuncture, herbs, and dietary and lifestyle advice in a traditional Chinese medicine consultation. The effect of studying each component separately or in combination as part of a whole system needs to be considered.[28]

According to Kleijnen and his colleagues, healing is an interactive process under three influences:

- the self-healing properties of the subject, which is the inherent self-healing force of vital energy from which the patient recovers entirely without the physician's intervention, rather than to some sort of active, intentional, purposeful arousal of a subject's optimal physiological, psychosomatic, and somatopsychic healing resources by the therapist;
- the nonspecific effects induced by the presence of the therapist and the therapeutic setting, like the nonpharmacologic benefits of the protocol involvement and of participants; and
- the specific effects of the physical or pharmacological therapeutic interventions in cases where "contextual factors contribute to a strong placebo response," due to "the potentiating or adjunctive effect of the placebo response." Placebos can be used to "potentiate the effect of an active treatment" that would have otherwise been far less effective. These effects are not isolated

mutually exclusive effects, and rather than just adding, they may help or hinder each other to various degrees.[29]

Therefore, the placebo effect, thought of as the result of the inert pill, can be better understood as an effect of the relationship between doctor and patient. Adding the doctor's caring to medical care affects the patient's experience of treatment, reduces pain, and may affect outcome.

Special attention to research design is therefore crucial. Strong collaborative teams of research scientists and unified integrative medicine practitioners are vital to effectively address such methodological concerns. Studies on the impact of healing methods need to assess the power of a whole system to evoke change in terms of outcomes that are meaningful to the healer and the patient in everyday life. They are not always intended to prove causality, test a specific theory or mechanism of action, or determine efficacy or effectiveness. Healing is complex, unitary, or ecological and participatory, and there may even be a nonlocal aspect.[30]

Therefore, the methods needed to study these approaches also must reflect this complexity.

Research methods need to be open, dynamic, interdependent, and participatory. They also need to reflect a multidimensional, longitudinal, contextual, and emergent process. Thus, an important research design challenge is to integrate pattern, structure, process, and meaning with the ways of knowing—personal, connected, and objective—all with appropriate methodology.

The important lesson is that CAM research needs not only specific skills and teamwork, but, in particular, prominent medical alliances. It requires a deliberate policy that supports a collegiate approach, whereby those involved in CAM and in conventional medicine genuinely communicate with each other to develop the research agenda.

However, according to the new unified integrative medicine, health and disease are redefined. Under the new definition, health and disease can be evaluated and measured with scientific and objective methods. The health depends upon two factors: resonance between the body's magnetic field and the organs and the vitality of the organs. The dissonance is created by unresolved psychological conflicts that have caused stress, leading to imbalance in the autonomic nervous system and increasing the sympathetic tone to the detriment of the parasympathetic. In measuring this balance, we can determine the degree of stress present in the person. The other parameter is the amount of available energy in the system. We know that the lack of energy results in reduced ATP availability of electrons, which causes the increase of oxidative stress and the increase of free radicals. Measuring oxidative stress provides us with clear information on the amount of energy available in the defense system.

The state of stress is based on the measurement of HRV (heart rate variability) to check the balance between the sympathetic and parasympathetic systems, while the state of vitality is evaluated through the measurement of pH and the oxidation-reduction potential of the blood. Additionally, the measurement of the electrical resistance at the acupuncture points may be useful to assess the state of stress and vitality in the meridians and, consequently, in the organs associated.

These measurements should be associated with all therapeutic interventions in order to verify the usefulness and effectiveness of any treatment.

This can be very useful for research and may be important to provide scientific value to the method.

What Is Life?

In order to understand health, we need to understand the basic components of life. According to our model, life is viewed as the integration of physical elements, which are guided by the laws of physics and chemistry, and vital energy, which is guided by the laws of electromagnetism and quantum physics. This energy confers the driving force of life and intelligence. The vital force is described by the classical law of electromagnetism, while intelligence and consciousness are described by the principles of quantum physics. To describe the whole spectrum of life, we should integrate the chemical laws that describe the interaction between physical elements, the laws of electromagnetism, the dynamics of life, and quantum physics, which describe the information differences and consciousness of the cells and complex organisms.

It is essential to have basic elements without which there would never be a life. The reductionist principle explains the interaction between different elements based on physics and chemistry. A number of reactions between different elements may occur in a collectively autocatalytic way to form more complex molecules, such as RNA, which has a paramount role in transmission, processing, and translation of genetic information. (A *set* of chemical reactions can be said to be "collectively autocatalytic" if a number of those reactions produce, as reaction products, catalysts for enough of the other reactions that the entire set of chemical reactions is self-sustaining given an input of energy and food molecules). However, the autocatalytic reaction is not casual but guided by the self-organization principle. The self-organization principle tells us that these interactions are organized in a coherent pattern where a structure or function appears in a system without an external element imposing it through planning. According to the holism and emergentism, the globally coherent pattern is due to the emergent property, which is more than the sum of the local interaction of the elements that make up the system. In fact, everything in the universe has a magnetic field around it; however, the emergent properties of all the magnetic fields of the composing system self-organize the system and become intelligently designed. The emergent property is a kind of energy that differentiates between animate and inanimate material and affords it attributes of life as it is in vitalism. Furthermore, the emergent property is intelligent and it is the force that designs the structure and guides the function of the organism, which is called intelligent design.

What Kind of Information Is This, and What Law of Physics Can Be Used to Describe It?

It should be the same information that guides the behavior of particles in the subnuclear level. This belongs to the quantum realm. Quantum mechanics is the body of scientific principles that explains the behavior of matter and its interactions with energy on the scale of atoms and atomic particles. The first axiom of quantum mechanics states that every system can be described by a wave function or quantum potential that is a function of all the particle coordinates and possibly the time. According to the uncertainty principle of Heisenberg, it is not possible to know the values of all of the properties of the system at the same time; those properties that are not known with precision must be described by probabilities. Therefore, the description of nature is essentially probabilistic. However, some physicists have argued that the state of a physical system, as formulated by quantum mechanics, does not give a complete description for the system (i.e., that quantum mechanics is ultimately incorrect and that a correct theory would provide descriptive categories to account for all observable behavior and thus avoid any indeterminism). Therefore, they proposed the hidden variable theories. Albert Einstein was the most famous proponent of hidden variables; he objected to the fundamentally probabilistic nature of quantum mechanics and famously declared, "I am convinced God does not play dice."

He express his idea in his private letter to Max Born, March 3, 1947:

> I admit, of course, that there is a considerable amount of validity in the statistical approach which you were the first to recognize clearly as necessary given the framework of the existing formalism. I cannot seriously believe in it because the theory cannot be reconciled with the idea that physics should represent a reality in time and space, free from spooky actions at a distance. ... I am quite convinced that someone will eventually come up with a theory whose objects, connected by laws, are not probabilities but considered facts, as used to be taken for granted until quite recently.

The first hidden-variable theory was the *pilot wave theory* of Louis de Broglie, dating from 1927. The currently best-known hidden-variable theory, the causal interpretation, of the physicist and philosopher David Bohm, formulated in 1952, is a nonlocal hidden-variable theory. Nowadays it is considered to be one of many interpretations of quantum mechanics, which give a realist interpretation and not merely a positivistic one to quantum-mechanical calculations. The de Broglie–Bohm theory is explicitly nonlocal. The velocity of any one particle depends on the value of the wave function, which depends on the whole configuration of the universe. Therefore, the concept of *quantum potential* was elaborated upon by Bohm and Basil Hiley to explain why and how the quantum particle behaves a certain way under the influence of the information potential and how the concept of a *quantum potential* leads to the notion of an "unbroken wholeness of the entire universe," proposing that the fundamental new quality introduced by quantum physics is nonlocality.[32]

The intelligent design is actually described by quantum physics as quantum potential. Basil and Hiley also called the quantum potential an *information potential*, given that it influences the form of processes and is itself shaped by the environment as a kind of "quantum Intelligence."[33]

Bohm's basic assumption is that "elementary particles are actually systems of extremely complicated internal structure, acting essentially as amplifiers of 'information' contained in a quantum wave." This hidden information is called "implicate order." The quantum potential constitutes an implicate (hidden) order and may itself be the result of yet a further implicate order (superimplicate order).[34]

The implicate order is the intelligent design that guides the particles and manifests as explicate order; it makes up our manifest world, which is secondary, derivative. It "flows out of the law of the Implicate Order." According to the theory, the particles are not the fundamental reality; the focus should be on discrete particle-like quanta in a continuous field, which connects everything with everything else. In principle, any individual element could reveal "detailed information about every other element in the universe." Thus, in Bohmian mechanics, the configuration of a system of particles evolves via a deterministic motion choreographed by the wave function.

Like the vitalism principle, Bohm believes that at the very depths of the ground of all existence exists a planum of immense background of energy. The energy of this ground is likened to one whole and unbroken movement called "holomovement," which carries the implicate order. If there is apparent evolution in the universe, it is because the different scales or dimensions of reality are already implicit in its structure. Bohm theorizes that the order in every immediately perceptible aspect of the world should be regarded as coming out of a more comprehensive implicate order, in which all aspects ultimately merge and can be describe as a quantum state. The quantum state is a set of mathematical variables that maximally describes the system; it is the expression of the implicate order. A quantum state can be either "pure" or "mixed." For example, the state of an electron within a hydrogen atom is pure, and it is given by its four quantum numbers, which are represented by a vector in a Hilbert space, which is a generalization of our more usual three-dimensional space. The living cell, for example, has a mixed quantum state, which is composed from another mixed quantum state of different elements, which has a pure quantum state of electrons. The quantum state of the living cell is the mathematical expression of the implicate order, which informs the different parts of the cell what structure and function to have. Each living cell has different probabilities of outcome, called probability distributions. These probability distributions arise for both mixed states and pure states: It is impossible in quantum mechanics (unlike classical mechanics) to have a state in which all properties of the system are fixed and certain. This is exemplified by the Heisenberg uncertainty principle and reflects a core difference between classical and quantum physics. Even in quantum theory, however, for every quantity, there are states that determine its value exactly. The fixed quantum state determines the properties of the heart cell, for example, guided by its location in the heart. The hepatic cell has a function and structure that are determined by its location in the liver. However, the liver cell still has a potential to be a different cell if the quantum state upon it changed and become similar to that of a colon cell. In this case, the cell will be called metastasis. Life is enfolded in the totality, and even when it is not manifest, it is somehow implicit.

This new concept reverses the self-organization concept based on the belief that structure or function appears in a system without a central authority, and the globally coherent pattern appears from the local interaction of the elements that make up the system. Instead, the quantum state of the cell is the central authority, and it is predetermined by its position in space as an implicate order even before the appearance of the cell, because it is a part of other supersystem. The behavior of each cell in the organ and every organ in the body is limited to the rules of the system, which are determined by its quantum state. The local interactions of the elements in the cell are guided by this implicate order of the quantum state.

Where Did Life Intelligence Come from?

The quantum state therefore is the intelligence of the cells. But what determines the quantum state of each cell?

In my book *The Seven Principles and the Seventh Sense*, I describe the universal principles and laws that guide everything in the universe. The seventh law is the universal code, which is considered the law of information and intelligence. It lies in the quantum realm; it informs the material how to be and how to behave and to evolve.

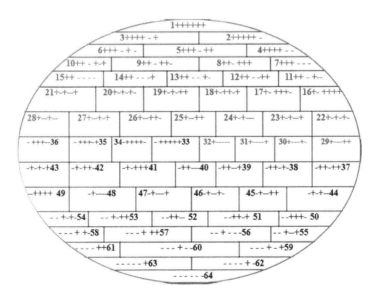

The universal code is derivative of the polar force. In quantum mechanics, every system has a magnetic charge with opposite characteristics at different points. Even atoms with similar electronegativity values can form a polar molecule, if they contain three or more atoms arranged nonsymmetrically. One end of the molecule has a small positive charge, and one end has a small negative charge. This arrangement of charges forms a dipole. The measurement of the strength of the dipole, called a *dipole moment*, depends on the size of the electrical charges, the distance between them, and how they are arranged. The arrangement of the molecules in the dipolar system and their dipole moment depend on the magnetic force in that specific location in the system. The molecular dipole moment in the space a certain distance between the two poles is a function of superposition of the two poles in different grades, which depends on the distance of each pole. (Each pole is composed of three vortices, and each one can be positive with spin up or negative with spin down.) Therefore, the superposition can be expressed as six signs, which are a representation of the sum of the sex vortices in space. There are sixty-four possible combinations of superposition of bipolar forces; each one of them corresponds to a quantum state that is encoded in one of the sixty-four codes (see "the Universal Code").

Each quantum state has a magnetic moment, which is a vector that characterizes the magnet's overall magnetic properties. Thus, every quantum system can be one of sixty-four possibilities, regardless of whether it is a macrocosm or a microcosm, in the material or the energetic system, in the animal, vegetable, or human world.

Each bipolar system can be expressed by one of these sixty-four codes. In each quantum state, we find sixty-four subquantum state, and each quantum state is a part of other superquantum states. This is the base for self-similar patterns of fractals and includes the idea of a detailed pattern repeating itself. In each system, each part is informed about the rest of the system in a nonlocal manner; this means that the information does not need photons, which are limited to the speed of light, to inform different part of the system with different information. All parts are informed instantaneously. The universal code is the intelligent and mathematical design. It lies in the quantum realm, which guides the behavior of the very elementary particles that constitute the material.

The living system, like our body, is a bipolar system that is guided by seven levels of superposition of quantum systems, where each tissue, each organ, and each cell is informed with a precise quantum state that is influenced by other external environmental information or internal information generated from beliefs, emotions, and thoughts.

Health, therefore, depends mainly on two factors: the magnetic field strength and quantum field information. The stronger the magnetic field, the more resistant to the internal and external influences it is.

The Vital Force of Living Cells

A living organism is considered to be a dissipative system that has a dynamic regime. In some sense, it is in a reproducible steady state. Thermodynamically, it is an open system, which is operating out of and often far from thermodynamic equilibrium in the environment with which it exchanges energy and matter, conferring a dynamic quality to the living organism. This quality that distinguishes living organisms from dead organisms and inanimate matter manifests in functions, such as metabolic activity, growth, proliferative activity, cellular repair, and regeneration is capable of movement, intracellular transport of nutrients, active cell-to-cell communication and response to stimuli or adaptation to the environment originating from within the organism. The energy status of cells, tissues, organs, and the whole body is defined by the cellular ability to produce and maintain threshold levels of cellular energy called adenosine triphosphate (ATP). Cells derive their energy from enzyme-catalyzed chemical reactions, which involves the oxidation of fats, proteins, and carbohydrates. Cells can produce energy by oxygen-dependent aerobic enzyme pathways and by less efficient fermentation pathways. The specialized proteins and enzymes involved in oxidative phosphorylation are located on the inner mitochondrial membrane and form a molecular respiratory chain or wire. This molecular wire (electron transport chain) passes electrons donated by several important electron donors through a series of intermediate compounds to molecular oxygen, which becomes reduced to water. In the process ADP is converted into ATP. When the electron donors of the respiratory chain, NADH and FADH2, release their electrons, hydrogen ions are also released. These positively charged hydrogen ions are pumped out of the mitochondrial matrix across the inner mitochondrial membrane, creating an electrochemical gradient. At the last stage of the respiratory chain, these hydrogen ions are allowed to flow back across the inner mitochondrial membrane, and they drive a molecular motor called ATP synthase in the creation of ATP like water drives a water wheel.[35]

This normal energy production process utilizes electron transport and hydrogen ion gradients across the mitochondrial membrane. If disrupted, the membrane potential will drop and cells become cancerous.

The cell is an electromagnetic entity charged with energy; therefore, it reacts to electric charges and magnetic momentum. Among the electrical properties that cells manifest are the ability to conduct electricity, create electrical fields, and function as electrical generators and batteries. In the body, electricity is carried by a number of mobile charge carriers as well as electrons. Electron semiconduction also takes place in biological polymers.[36]

The body uses the exterior cell membrane and positively charged mineral ions which are maintained in different concentrations on each side of the cell membrane to create a cell membrane potential. Trans-membrane potential refers to the voltage difference across a cell's bilayer membrane that is established by the balance of intracellular and extracellular ionic concentrations. All animal cells are surrounded by a plasma membrane composed of a lipid b_layer with a variety of types of proteins embedded in it. Such a balance is maintained via passive and active ion transport through various ion channels and transporters located within the membrane. The membrane potential in a cell derives ultimately from two factors: electrical force and diffusion. Electrical force arises from the mutual attraction between particles with opposite electrical charges (positive and negative) and the mutual repulsion between particles with the same type of charge (either positive or negative). Diffusion arises from the statistical tendency of particles to redistribute from regions where they are highly concentrated to regions where the concentration is low (due to thermal energy). According to traditional membrane potential theory, the resting membrane potential of a cell is achieved when the electrochemical forces driving ion movement are equalized and ionic equilibrium is maintained. Maintenance of ionic homeostasis is a critical feature of cell viability and metabolism.[37-38]

Surprising specificity has been uncovered in the relationship between changes in levels of membrane potential and alteration of cell function. Furthermore, increasing evidence has pointed toward not only a correlation but a functional relationship between membrane potential and cell functions, such as proliferation and differentiation. It has long been observed that membrane potential levels are tightly correlated with cell proliferation-related events, such as mitosis, DNA synthesis, and overall cell cycle progression. Virtually all eukaryotic cells (including cells from animals, plants, and fungi) maintain a nonzero transmembrane potential, usually with a negative voltage in the cell interior as compared to the cell exterior. The membrane potential has two basic functions. First, it allows a cell to function as a battery, providing power to operate a variety of "molecular devices" embedded in the membrane. Second, in electrically excitable cells, such as neurons and muscle cells, it is used for transmitting signals between different parts of a cell. Signals generated by the opening or closing of ion channels at one point in the membrane produce a local change in the membrane potential that causes electric current to flow rapidly to other points in the membrane.

Several studies have demonstrated that every healthy organism has its typical membrane potential that evolves and diminishes with aging and disease. Different organs have different membrane potentials, and this influences their biological function. Resting potentials of various cell types fall within a wide range (generally –10 mV to –90 mV), and cells' positions along such a membrane potential scale generally correspond to their proliferative potential.[39]

However, resting potentials of normal nonproliferative cells range between -36 mV and -95 mV. Somatic cells that have a high degree of polarization (a hyperpolarized membrane potential) tend to be quiescent and do not typically undergo mitosis. Conversely, developing cells and cancerous cells tend to have a smaller degree of polarization (a depolarized membrane potential below -36 mV) and are mitotically active.[40-41]

Collectively, the data demonstrate that bioelectric properties can serve as markers for cell characterization and can control cell mitotic activity, cell cycle progression, aging, and differentiation.

In cancerous tissue, the electrical potential of cell membranes is maintained at a lower level than that of healthy cells and electrical connections are disrupted. Membrane potential disappearance will lead inevitably to death. Therefore, membrane potential is vital in order to maintain life and life functions.

We can summarize that the electromagnetic field plays a cardinal role in life. It can be considered as a promoter of life and secondary to biochemical activity. Its measurement should be used to evaluate the vitality and life strength. Its absence will lead to inevitable death.

The emergent magnetic field from the electromagnetic activity of the cells is the blueprint that governs all processes of life. It has two main roles:

1) information and communication in that they are employed by living organisms as information conveyors from the environment to the organism, within the organism, and among organisms, and
2) life's vital processes in that they facilitate pattern formation, organization, and growth control within the organism.[42]

Resonance and Vitality

Two physical concepts should be understood before we start to redefine the basic concepts of health and disease: vitality and resonance.

In order to understand how the psyche influences the physical body and activates neurons in the brain to secrete neuropeptides and how fear contracts the abdomen, etc., we should first understand how energy affects matter.

According to Einstein's famous equation, $E = mc^2$, the energy, E, of a physical system is numerically equal to the product of its mass, m, and the speed of light, c, squared. Mass and energy are the same property of physical systems, but the conversion of mass into energy (or vice versa) is a genuine physical process. Matter has both mass and energy, whereas fields only have energy. However, since the equivalence of mass and energy entails that mass and energy are really the same physical property after all, one can no longer distinguish between matter and fields, as they now have both mass *and* energy.

The Planck-Einstein relation $E = h\upsilon$ describes the relationship between energy and frequency, where E = energy, h = Planck's constant, and υ = frequency. Changing the frequency will change the energy and consequently the mass as well, according to the equation:

$$\Delta E = \Delta m \; c^2$$

where ΔE designates a change in the energy of a system and Δm designates a change in the mass of the system. If we divide both sides by c^2, we can see that if the energy changes by an amount ΔE, its mass changes concurrently by an amount $\Delta m = \Delta E/c^2$.

Changing the frequency of the body will change the mass, which means changing the basic properties of the physical matter that appears as a disease. The psyche is found in the quantum realm; it acts directly on the magnetic field by changing the magnetic moment. Therefore, changing the energetic frequency of the psyche directly influences the body's magnetic moment through the energy of the soul (magnetoelectric field), which connects psyche and body.

This interaction between the psyche and the physical body is described using physical terms, such as *wave interference*, which occurs when two waves meet while traveling along the same medium. The interference of waves between the quantum realm of the psyche and magnetic field of the physical body causes the medium, which is the physical body, to take on a shape that results from the net effect of the two individual waves upon the particles of the body. Normally, when we feel harmony and well-being, there is a constructive wave interference between the soul and the physical body and that interference shapes and guides the physiological reaction, genetic expression, and metabolic reactions. Constructive interference takes place when the two interfering waves have a displacement in the same direction. In this case, both waves have an upward displacement; consequently, the medium has an upward displacement that is greater than the displacement of the two interfering pulses. This results in increasing the basic vital energy of the cells. Constructive interference is observed at any location where the two interfering waves are displaced upward or displaced downward. Destructive interference instead is a type of interference that occurs at any location along the medium where the two interfering waves have a displacement in opposite directions. For instance, when two pulses with opposite displacements (i.e., one pulse displaced up and the other down) meet at a given location, the upward pull of one pulse is balanced (canceled or destroyed) by the downward pull of the other pulse. The result is that the two pulses completely destroy each other when they are completely overlapped. At the instant of complete overlap, there is no resulting displacement of the particles of the medium. This can lead to changing the frequency of the body's energy and the amplitude of the wave. The two interfering waves do not need to have equal amplitudes in opposite directions for destructive interference to occur. For example, a pulse with a maximum displacement of +1 unit could meet a pulse with a maximum displacement of -2 units. The resulting displacement of the medium during complete overlap is -1 unit. This is still destructive interference since the two interfering pulses have opposite displacements. In this case, the destructive nature of the interference does not lead to complete cancellation.

Psychological trauma and conflicts change the energy frequency of the soul and create a state of dissonance between the soul and the body; this kind of dissonance creates destructive wave interference and weakens the vital energy of the tissues, which could appear as organic disease.

The same concept can be expressed in musical terms. *Consonance* and *dissonance* are related to constructive and destructive wave interference correspondently. In more general usage, a *consonance* is a combination of notes that sounds pleasant to most people when played at the same time; *dissonance* is a combination of notes that sounds harsh or unpleasant to most people. It is worthy to note that this is a relative cultural concept since Western artistic music tradition can sound dissonant to Balkan, Arabic, or Chinese listeners and vice versa.

The psychological conflict is individual; it is related to the person's culture and traditions as well as personal beliefs and individual needs. The sense of conflict in the first place is due to the state of dissonance that creates unpleasant destructive wave interference and suffering that can lead finally to disease. The same sensation can be provoked when we hear dissonant music, as expressed by Roger Kamien: "An unstable tone combination is a dissonance; its tension demands an onward motion to a stable chord. Thus dissonant chords are 'active'; traditionally they have been considered harsh and have expressed pain, grief, and conflict."[31]

The Science of the Soul

What is soul and how can we define it scientifically? Every human being is a biological complex subjected to the energy forces, which direct and guide its physiological, metabolic, genetic, and psychological functions. These energies are called collectively a *soul*.

The energy forces are of three types:

1. a force inherited from our parents called the *animal soul*
2. a quantum state of divine spiritual energy gained during or shortly before delivery called the *human soul*
3. a quantum state of divine spiritual energy gained in the time of attribution of the name, called the *guiding spirit*

The *animal soul* is formed at the moment of fertilization when the single sperm encounters the egg and a bipolar force is formed.

The human soul gets to the physical body at the birth moment when the newborn takes the first breath. This is called *inspiration*, which means "in spirit."

The spirit guide joins the newborn when its name is pronounced.

a. The animal soul

We can define the animal soul as the *unifying and integrating essence that creates an indivisible whole between body, psyche, and spirit. It is the source of life, self-nourishment, growth, decay, movement, rest, perception, sensation, emotions, and instinctive intellect, and it is the primary motivation in life.*

The animal soul has three parts:

1. the vegetative soul, which is made of two major poles and a magnetoelectric field or aura
2. the sensitive soul, which is made of seven chakras
3. the intellectual soul, which is made of twelve double meridians

1. The Vegetative Soul

The vegetative soul is made of **two poles which I called the major poles and a magnetic field**. In order to understand the effect of energy on living organisms, we will take the example of a worm. If we measure the electrical potential on the extremities, we find that the head has a positive electrical potential, while the tail is negative. Its two poles are thus localized, the negative near the head, the positive one near the tail. The energy passage from the two poles takes place through the body, causing a wave of contraction and release similar to the peristaltic movement in the intestine, and, in fact, this movement accurately represents the energetic movement and makes it visible on the worm's body.

The bipolarity of the human body starts with the union between the positive polarity spermatozoon and the ovule, with its negative polarity. Little by little, as the fetus develops, polarity is organized not only at the cellular level but also at the organ level and at the level of the whole body until it reaches the male's positive polarity and the female's negative one. Male and female both have two poles with different dispositions with opposite poles in the female relative to the male.

The inside of the body has negative polarity, like inside the cell. The external is positive. The front of the body is receptive, negative, while the rear is active, positive; the left-hand side of the body is negative, while the right-hand side is positive. Internal organs, too, have their own polarity, and each organ is considered as a pole for another organ. For example, the heart, the liver, the pancreas, the spleen, the lungs, and the kidneys have negative polarity, while the small intestine, the gall bladder, the stomach, the large intestine, and the urinary bladder have positive polarity.

The organs have complementary polar properties; for example, the lungs and the large intestine have opposite and complementary polar properties, and the same happens with the heart and the small intestine, the bladder and the kidneys, the gall bladder and the liver, etc. Only the brain is bipolar by itself, because the negative pole is present in the right hemisphere, while the positive pole is in the left one.

The location of the negative pole on the left- or right-hand side depends on the sex; whether a person is right-handed or left-handed can be inverted in different situations, such as after castration, menopause, hormonal contraception treatment, etc. This inversion could create certain conditions favorable to the appearance of mental disturbances due to energy weakness.

The central nervous vegetative system is divided into two opposing functional and polar systems, which are the sympathetic systems, with positive male polarity related to force, stress, contracting, and the parasympathetic system and negative female polarity related to calmness, expansion, and relaxation.

The peripheral nervous system is functionally divided into two parts, which function one in respect of the other, the *motor* innervation and the *sensitive* innervation, each of which is divided, in turn, in two other fragments. The motor innervation is divided into *vegetative motor* of smooth muscles (peristaltic) and the *motor or striated muscles* (ambulation and movement). The sensitive innervation is divided into *vegetative sensibility* (stomach, intestine, etc.) and the *dermal and muscular sensitivity.* Each innervation—peripheral or central, sensitive or motor, comprises two parts with inverse polarity, one in respect of the other: afferent nerves, with an energy flow from the center to the periphery and efferent nerves, from the periphery to the center.

In Chinese medicine, for example, the ten vital organs are grouped into five pairs, so that the center of each is an organ with negative polarity—"solid" yin and one organ with positive polarity, "empty" yang. One could say that yin organs are more vital than yang, and their dysfunction creates major health problems in human beings. Organs are not coupled arbitrarily but linked by concrete functional and anatomic connections. However, the theory traditional Chinese medicine failed to describe is the presence of major poles that are the source of the meridians and the magnetic field.

• The Major Poles

Despite the great discoveries of the ancient Chinese about the chi, especially the meridians and their trajectories inside and outside the body, they failed to discover the presence of the major poles. In fact, the meridian designs vanish somewhere inside the body without knowing what originates them and what maintains their flow.

For me, it was obvious to think that every polar phenomenon should have poles. I started to research a notion about the poles and never found one. When I applied the energy model (see the *Seven Principles and the Seventh Sense*), I could see that the poles of the model are localized in the chest and in the pelvis. The discovery of the internal structure of the poles could explain to me the energetic nature of meridians, their number, the reason for their flow direction, and the complementarity between meridians, the magnetic field, and the chakras. The magnetic poles are the energy dynamo that generate the dynamics; they push and pull the energy from the center to the periphery and vice versa.

Each living organism has two poles, which are pure energy, without physical correspondence in the body. The same phenomenon of the poles exists in magnets. That is the reason why when the magnet is cut into two smaller magnets, new poles appear and the original poles are displaced.

Each one of us has two poles that I call the *major poles*: the north pole, which is located deep in the center of the thorax, and the south pole, which is located deep inside the abdomen, approximately 2.5 to 4 centimeters under the navel.

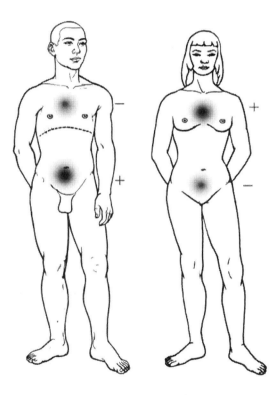

I prefer to call them north and south poles and not negative and positive poles, because they have different configurations. Each of the poles can be positive or negative. I call the poles major to distinguish them from other poles related to the seven subsystems, such as the nervous system, respiratory system, cardio-circulatory and lymphatic system, digestive system, kidneys and urinary system, musculoskeletal system, and sexual and reproductive system. The emergent magnetic of all systems together form the major poles and main magnetic field.

In general terms, in women, the north pole is positive and the south pole is negative, while in men, it is the other way round (i.e., the north pole is negative and the south pole positive). The thoracic pole is considered to be the seat of the spirit, and there inhabits our spiritual will, which guides us throughout our lives, and there we also find all that we would like to be, do, or become, from the most insignificant moment or thing in our life to the highest values thereof [our life].

On the other hand, in the south pole, inhabits our intention, and there we store energy and force. For individuals practicing martial arts, this is the point of origin of all movements. By means of this pole, the healers connect with the earth's energy core and synchronize with the earth the vibration of their body. Thus, they extract energy from the earth field to restore balance and health to the sick.

Furthermore, in this pole is stored the sexual energy from tantric sexual practices in order to use this energy for all life tasks from thinking clearly and having physical force, sexual vigor, and good health.

Tantra, born in India more than six thousand years ago, emerged as a rebellion against organized religion, which held that sexuality should be rejected in order to reach enlightenment. The word *Tantra* means "to manifest, to expand, to show and to weave." In this context, sex is thought to expand consciousness and to weave together the polarities of male (represented by the Hindu god Shiva) and female (embodied by the Hindu goddess Shakti) into a harmonious whole. Couples need not adopt the tantric pantheon in order to benefit from the sexual wisdom of this ancient art. Tantric sexual practices teach us to prolong the act of making love and to utilize potent orgasmic energies more effectively in order to charge the battery and maintain a healthy life.

In a healthy person, both poles are aligned by means of a central straight line when the back or spine is held straight. This alignment leads to a synchronization between our intentions and our spiritual mission in life. Thus, we shall be synchronized with the whole, we shall have a large share of integrity, force, and personal purpose, for we shall be synchronized with the universal purpose. Then we can enjoy life to the fullest, because we can understand its meaning, the true sense of happiness, luck, and well-being.

When this aligning between the two poles is lacking, there shall be no synchronization and a contradiction shall appear between the individual's personal intentions and his or her spiritual mission. Suffering and bad luck shall fill his life. Since there shall be no synchronization with the basic personal nature, he or she shall be lacking in spontaneity and intuition, and this will create an internal conflict that will be expressed in the form of arguments with others.

The human body is subject to changes in the polar force due to the influence of complex internal and external factors, such as, for example, the weather, geographical location, seasons, temperature, colors, kinds of food, the taste of the food, emotions, etc.—phenomena over which the body has no influence.

The Development of the Major Poles

Polarity explains to us simply the phenomena that are sometimes considered mysterious and very hard to explain otherwise. Let us take, for example, the ovum fertilized by the sperm.

The attraction between the sperm and the ovum stems from the opposing polar force existing between these two cells and also manifesting in their electromagnetic potential. The sperm has positive polarity that characterizes all the cell nuclei, since most of it comprises a nucleus and a tail with very little cytoplasm. In contrast, most of the ovum comprises cytoplasm and is generally characterized by negative polarity. The attraction between the two cells is pure polar magnetic attraction.

A fertilized ovule is called zygote. It maintains these two poles separate (i.e., the male positive pole and the female negative pole) and the force generated between them is the dynamic base of cell multiplication and embryonic development.

This explains the difficulty women sometimes have becoming pregnant, despite the fact that, medically, the anatomical structure and physiological functioning are correct. A drop in the level of vitality of one or both partners will be manifested in a decline in the polar power of attraction that inhibits or prevents insemination. The fertilized egg will lack the strength to embed itself in the womb and develop into an embryo.

The fertilization process is affected by the balance between the male and the female energies. An excess of male energy in one of the parents, especially the woman, will result in the sperm cells that contain the Y chromosome enjoying priority over the sperm cells with the X chromosomes, a process that will determine the sex of the embryo as male. During the first stages of the pregnancy, the embryo's development is significantly affected by the amount of the mother's estrogen. This hormone is excreted in a quantity proportional to the male energy existing in the woman. The amount of male energy can also affect the development of male embryos, since the female embryo needs female energy in order to cause the female facets to develop.

The embryo—and thereafter the fetus—is affected by the degree of balance between the male and female energies. Thus, the mother's love charges the female pole (of the son or daughter) while the father's love charges the male pole. Food also affects the polar balance since it also has male and female polarity. Foods originating in seeds, such as almonds and legumes, or root vegetables, such as carrots, garlic, onions, and ginseng, as well as fish and meat, have male polarity, strengthen the male energy, and increase sexual drive as aphrodisiacs by raising the level of testosterone in the blood. In contrast, vegetables that grow on the surface of the ground, fruit (without seeds), and milk enjoy female polarity.

After birth and later, during the child's development, both poles shall be fed by each of the parents.

During pregnancy, the fetus develops with an excess of female energy and is thus female in its attributes and characterized by the physical and energetic receptive attributes.

After birth and during the child's growth, the two poles are fed by the parents. The mother's love (or that of another woman) will feed the female pole, and the father's love (or that of another male in the family) will feed the male pole.

There is a dynamic cycle during the poles' development where the energy is dominant in one of the poles every three years until twelve years. One pole shall have its maximum energy content and shall determine how the child shall behave, especially when alternating attraction toward his or her parents. Therefore, in the first twelve years, we notice a variation of attraction and repulsion between the child and parents.

Thus, polarity is a dynamic phenomenon that changes every seven years until the age of twenty-one, explaining the physical, hormonal, and emotional changes that occur every seven years. So, after birth, the father's love will enrich this male energy, resulting in a balance between the two poles that peaks at the age of seven. From the ages of seven to fourteen, typical gender attributes begin to develop and sexual drive begins to manifest, which will fully mature by the age of fourteen. The polarity between the genders will intensify between the ages of fourteen and twenty-one. At the age of twenty-one and close to the cessation of physical growth, the main poles close. The energetic potency in both poles at this age affords the energetic, physical, sexual, and emotional potential for the rest of life.

The love received from parents during development is highly important, because it will determine the strength of the battery necessary for life. This energy is actually the source of basic vitality and will determine the basic behavior of adults, either at a self-realization level or in their intimate affective relations or their sexual relations, and their energy level necessary for health and longevity.

An unbalanced energy supply from the parents during the development period of childhood will be the cause of many behavioral and health disturbances.

An unbalance between the poles can be caused by two conditions:

1. an excess of energy
2. lack of energy

The excess of energy can be in one pole; therefore, the unbalance will lead the person to be attracted to situations that could lead to better balance. The excess of one pole could be related to a lack of love from one parent. Lack of love from both parents will lead to weakness, depression, and lack of sexual drive.

The sexual attraction is directly related to the opposite disposition of the poles between a couple and the strength of the magnetic potential. The opposite layout of the poles in both sexes creates an attraction of magnetic type and intense energy flow between the two sexes and manifests during sexual intercourse passing through four phases: excitement, expansion, orgasm, contraction, and relaxation.

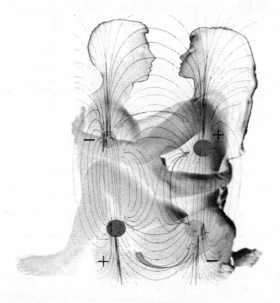

The energy flow direction determines the physiological nature of sexual function (i.e., in man, the flow goes from his positive south pole toward the woman's receptive negative south pole and from his south pole to the positive north pole in the thorax and from there to the negative north pole of the male's thorax). A loving woman gives love from her chest and receives sexual love in her genitals, while a loving man receives love in this chest and provides sexual love.

This process aims to achieve a polar energy balance in order to be able to maintain homeostasis and to have a state of well-being healthily in all other aspects of life and spiritual fulfillment.

A basic unbalance between the south and the north pole due to an unbalanced supply of male or female energy during the various development stages up and until sexual adulthood could create a disturbance in the individual's sexual behavior, such as homosexuality, especially if it is associated with emotional conflict with one or both parents.

The Difference between Male and Female

What is the difference between a man and a woman, between babies of either gender, boy or girl? This question bothered and continues to concern scientists, biologists, psychologists, and philosophers. Behind the attempt to understand the differences and find their source is our desire as parents, caregivers, and educators to know how to handle these differences, to exploit the talents typical of each gender, and to translate them into achievements in all areas of life.

The fact that boys and girls were not born the same is very hard to disguise, at least not physically and genetically. But to what extent does this fact affect the differences in behavior and the talents of each gender? Are these differences objective and inborn, or are they the result of environmental influences, such as parental attitude, education, and society?

The answers are not unequivocal. There are studies that claim the differences are inborn; some ascribe the cause for the differences between the genders to social behavior, and others can be interpreted in either direction. At the same time, one can note three differences that enjoy reliable research validity and can bear witness to the innate differences between males and females:

- Spatial orientation ability, including the mental rotation ability, is better among males (i.e., they are better at performing assignments that demand finding identical two-dimensional or three-dimensional shapes rapidly and with maximum exactitude). This ability provides them with an advantage in areas such as engineering and geography.

- Far more males suffer from learning disorders, such as dyslexia, dysgraphia, and attention problems and from speech disabilities.
- The percentage of males who are mathematical geniuses is significantly higher than among females. In general, males are better at mathematics while females are superior in the verbal field.

Other attributes are also ascribed to males and females that have no research basis. Males are restless, powerful, and energetic; females are more disciplined, obedient, and can concentrate better.

Furthermore, the differences between the genders can be explored using the polar phenomena that also include sexuality. Thus, for example, the audio and smell senses of baby girls are more developed and the sense of touch of two-dimensional things is better, while baby boys have greater physical ability and better ability to touch three-dimensional objects.

Concentration, attention, and good receptivity are attributes that characterize female energy; therefore, girls are better balanced energetically, as for example in absorbing languages. The spatial ability of males stems from the expansion of the male energy, preparing them for professions, such as geography, engineering, and spatial orientation.

Not every male must behave exactly according to his genetic attributes since his behavior is determined by the balance between male and female energy. Thus, for example, a boy with excess female energy will be weaker physically, will not like physical activity, will play games based on receptivity, will have a gift for languages and art, and will have developed intuition. A girl with excess male energy will play games with boys that require physical strength, such as football and tennis. Her body will be strong and muscular; she will have a small bust and be hirsute from a young age. Her areas of interest will be computers, mathematics, and the exact sciences.

One can intervene and attain a balance between the poles in a way that will be suitable to the child's gender. Thus, for example, it is worth offering a boy who tends toward quiet female games male foods, such as legumes, almonds, fish, and meat in order to strengthen the male energy and allowing him to spend more time with his father or brothers. The male food of a girl with excess male energy should be reduced and her female food increased.

To sum up: the polar force is power that propels life. Dynamic balance in polar strength will preserve essential harmony and the free flow in life. Reciprocal relations between opposing poles, in all areas of life, will result in dynamics, activity, and development. Therefore, instead of judging and rejecting the negative aspect, we recommend using the dynamics created between the negative and the positive, the female and the male, the good and the bad, as a lever for progress and development.

The Origin of Homosexuality

Everything that exists in the world has only two states,
one normal and one abnormal, and both depend on a
single motive: they cannot exist without a reason.
—Charaka

There is no consensus among scientists about why a person develops
a particular sexual orientation, and the converging scientific findings
suggest that exclusive homosexuality is not a "lifestyle choice" but a
perfectly natural sexual orientation. While there is still much debate on the
exact causes of homosexuality and a "gay gene" remains elusive, biological
scientists still believe that there is a strong genetic influence to gayness.

From twin studies, there are indications that homosexuality is related
to something in the family not yet defined. Furthermore, biologists
have discovered forms of homosexuality in many other animal species
to which humans are related to varying degrees, from baboons to
dolphins and from penguins to worms. These are reasonably strong
claims that homosexuality is part of someone's genotype; there is still
much speculation as to how it got there. Different theories hypothesized
the relation between love deficiencies from parents and homosexuality;
however, none of the existing theories takes into consideration the
energy aspect related to parenteral love and environmental influences.

There are differences between being homosexual and gay. Not
every homosexual is gay, and not every gay person is homosexual.

Homosexuality means practicing sex with the same gender, which could be done to satisfy sexual desire in the absence of the opposite gender like in the military or prison. Sometimes, it is done because of impotence that appears when practicing sex with the opposite sex, when refuting the opposite gender, or because of romantic attraction and sexual excitation for the same gender.

For gay people, we intend a real need for the same gender with the impossibility of practicing sex for psychological refusal.

There are four types of homosexuals:

- male homosexual (bisexual) with an excess of female energy and lack of male energy
- male homosexual (gay) with an excess of male energy and lack of female energy associated with maternal conflict
- female homosexual (lesbian bisexual) with an excess of male energy and lack of female energy
- female homosexual (lesbian gay) with an excess of female energy and lack of male energy and blocked sexual conflict (with a father or other male)

According to this new vision, I can redefine homosexuality as *a biological necessity that is meant to restore the polar energy balance and homeostasis.*

Let us see some examples to understand better.

A male child who has not received male-type energy because of the absence of fatherly love may have an excess of female energy (i.e., the north pole will be charged while the south pole will be empty). In order to arrive at a balance, it is necessary to charge the male south pole, because when reaching adulthood under these conditions, he will never be able to have sexual contact with a woman—for this would imply a further loss of energy from his south pole and would worsen his energy imbalance and depression. This man will be impotent in his relations with women with similar polarity and will be attracted to other persons with excess male energy. This constitution is the basis of female-type homosexuality (receiver). However, these fellows can have successful sexual relations with females who have excess male energy. These females can be identified by their short hair, small breasts, and narrow pelvis.

In 1995, a forty-two-year old man arrived at my office suffering pains in the lower part of his back. He was generally healthy, except for some urinary infection episodes. During his energy check, using the blinking technique, I found the sexual center blocked. I found that his block could be traced down to 1987. After my questions, I confirmed that precisely that year he had had a sexual conflict with a woman because she had cheated on him, and from then on, he had no more sexual relations and felt that this conflict was responsible for his abstinence. Controlling the energy state of his poles, I discovered that his male positive pole was almost fully lacking in energy, and the patient confirmed that his relationship with his father had always been very conflictive and that even as a child he felt that he had not received love from his father. When I inquired into the relationship with his former girlfriend, he revealed that he had never been able to have sexual relations with her, in spite of several attempts. This man was not homosexual because he had repressed his tendencies but because he felt continuously in discomfort.

A child who grows up without maternal energy will have in his or her female north pole a very low amount of energy; on the other hand, his or her male south pole will be overloaded. In order to reach a balance, he or she will require a great amount of female [maternal] love. Such a man will be sexually potent only when he is deeply loved by the woman chosen by him, who shall provide him continuously with female love. If this man has had an emotional conflict, such as for example rage or even hate toward his mother, by whom he has been abandoned or abused, he will develop an abandonment conflict that will be expressed as an energy block in the center of his chest and which will prevent access by the female energy to his north pole. Now, in order to reach a balance in this case, the man feels the need to sexually discharge the energy excess from his south pole. True, a sexual relation with a woman will discharge the excess of energy in his south pole, but this will bring him to a very low energy level, which could impair his well-being and his health and could lead him to impotence. Now he will be attracted by another man, with whom he may only discharge a small amount of energy due to the minimum energy difference existing between him and another homosexual of the female type. This man will thus be a homosexual of the active male type.

Let's now analyze female homosexuality.

A woman who as a child has had an excess of paternal love as compared to maternal love because of the lack of a mother for different reasons will have her male positive pole much more charged than the female pole. Sexual contact with a man with an excess of male energy will worsen her unbalance. She will feel nervous and unsatisfied. However, she will be attracted to other women who can supply her with the female energy she is lacking and thus will have lesbian tendencies of the donating type. Furthermore, she will feel attracted to a romantic man who has an excess of female energy. In this case, she will be a bisexual lesbian.

A woman who as a child received a lot of female energy from her mother and nothing or very little from her father or had sexual abuse or rape from her father or another man has a basic repulsion to the man figure.

Even though she needs male energy, she cannot receive it from a male but from a female with excess male energy. This is a lesbian female gay.

On the other hand, a woman who has enjoyed only maternal love because of the lack of a father or some substitute shall have an excess of female-type energy and lack of male energy without having a conflict with her father or other male figure. In order to reach an energy balance, she will feel the need of male energy, which can be supplied through sexual contact. But since sexual contact does not repair the basic imbalance but rather offers a relatively short balance, the woman shall feel a need for frequent sexual contacts in order to feel balanced and satisfied, and thus we are facing a woman with nymphomaniac tendencies. If the lack of a father is accompanied by a conflict pervaded by hate toward him—either due to sexual abuse or any other motive—this woman will have her chest center closed and thus will never be able to receive love from another man. In this case, the only way to reach an energy balance will be by applying the surplus female energy to another woman who requires it, and thus we find an male lesbian.

What would happen if both had low-energy poles? Let us see a few examples:

A thirty-four-year-old woman arrived at my office because she had been suffering manic-depressive psychosis, which prevented her from leading a regular social life or continuing her studies at the university despite the medication prescribed by her psychiatrist.

When I checked the energy status of her two poles, I found a very low energy content, and then upon inquiring into her life as a child and as a teenager, I discovered that she had grown up in the midst of a family very poor in affection and love. The lack of love from both parents would cause an energy weakening of both poles, leading to an energy and bodily state of slowed-down vitality. She adopted dissociative reactions to traumas and conflicts because she had not enough energy to face the events. This was a facilitating factor to be exposed to the external influences of the spiritual entities.

There are intermediate situations in which there is no manifest lack of maternal or paternal love, but only a partial lack of one of the parent's love, leading to a slight imbalance, which can be easily controlled.

This was the case of a twenty-four-year-old girl who succeeded in having sexual intercourse with her boyfriend only when her best girlfriend was in bed with them; as long as this situation persisted (accepted by all three), she could have satisfactory relations with her boyfriend. They decided to get married and therefore left her girlfriend because of jealousy. She was unable to have sexual intercourse with her boyfriend. Thus, they separated.

This girl had a certain imbalance in her female south pole due to a lack of maternal love, and when she absorbed energy from her friend, she succeeded in striking a balance, and only then was she able to reach a satisfactory energy exchange with her boyfriend.

Another woman who had married for the second time and had no children came to me because of her infertility problem, which was due to lack of ovulation.

When examining the energy in the major poles, I felt that her female south pole was almost absent because of its very low energy content. As a child, she had been abandoned by her parents (at the time she was only two) and then she had been brought up by the grandfather who, by nurturing her north pole, compensated for the lack of male energy. Then, checking her husband, I discovered that he, too, had been abandoned by his parents as a child. This couple felt good together because, in spite of the woman's male energy excess, the husband did not have sufficient male energetic force to cause rejection between both. The lack of female energy was clearly manifested in the organs that need this energy for their function, such as ovaries and uterus. Thus, she lacked the necessary energy to produce ovulation and ripening of the ovule.

This woman had a polar constitution of the male lesbian type. Immediately after her first marriage, she discovered could not have intimate relations with her husband and she then got a divorce. With her second husband, she found a better balance due to the weakening of her husband's male pole. This allowed her not to be repelled by intimate relations; however, the sexual drive of both was low, to say the least, and this hampered fertilization even more, when taking into account that they only had sexual relations once or at a maximum twice per month.

2. The Sensitive Soul

The soul is represented by the seven energy centers called *chakras* in Hindu and tantric/yogic traditions. Chakras are part of the magnetic field. Various scriptural texts and teachings present a different number of chakras. There are many chakras in the subtle human body, according to the tantric texts; however, if we know the real nature of these chakras, we understand that there are only seven These chakras actually are vortices in the magnetic field formed due to suction of a part of the magnetic field by the endocrine glands. In fact, their name derives from the Sanskrit word for "wheel," but in the yogic context, a better translation of the word is "vortex or whirlpool."

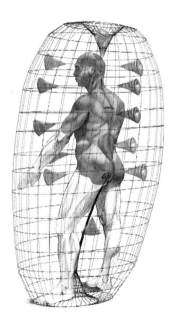

The apex of the chakra is found in the physical body, while its basis is found in the external limit of the magnetic field, and thus the larger the aura, the farther shall it be from the base of the energy center of the physical body.

The energy absorbed from the energy center supplies the required energy for hormonal secretion from a given gland, but also for all the organs in that given segment, such as, for example, the third center supplies energy not only to the pancreas but to all abdominal organs as well.

A lot of confusion about the chakras and their location, colors, and functions exists. The universal principles allow to us to understand better the different energy aspects, functions, and relations to emotional crises.

Seven chakras are located in seven different segments, which are separated with fibromuscular membranes to prevent the reciprocal influences. The energy absorbed by the chakra feeds also the endocrine gland coupled to the corresponding segment.

How are the energy centers connected with the endocrine glands? It seems that the high electromagnetic conductivity creates a zone of lower electromagnetic resistance that easily absorbs energy, and this energy suction forms the vortex in the magnetic field.

Each chakra is related to a certain frequency, increasing from the bottom toward the top, and is in harmony with the colors in the rainbow, so that the first center furnishes energy in harmony with red, the second with the color orange, the third with yellow, and so on down to the seventh center.

Thanks to these centers, humans interact with the external environment and react through the endocrine system. We perceive life in all its aspects through these energy centers, which are related to the endocrine glands that direct the physiological functions of the whole organism. Each energy center is linked to an aspect of our life. Psychological conflicts find their specific address in the corresponding zone. An internal or external stimulus that is perceived as a threat to the psychophysical integrity creates a defensive reaction and blocks the corresponding center. The endocrine gland that is nourished by that energy center begins to suffer and reacts to the stimulus by creating a physical knot or losing its vitality and therefore its physiological function.

The first segment is localized in the retroperitoneal space, where the kidneys and suprarenal glands are also located. The urogenital diaphragm separates it from the second segment, while the peritoneum separates it from the third segment.

The second chakra, related to orange, is connected to testicles in males and ovaries in females. The second segment and the pelvic or urogenital one comprises the prostate, bladder, and other glands linked to the sexual function of the male, while in the female, we find the uterus, the whole genital apparatus, and the bladder.

The third chakra, which is connected to the pancreas, is related to yellow. The third segment, which is localized in the abdominal area, includes the following organs: liver, spleen, and all the gastrointestinal tract from the stomach down to the sigmoid colon, the last part of the colon before the rectum. The breathing diaphragm and its upper boundary separate it from the fourth segment, while the peritoneum separates it from the first segments and the urogenital diaphragm from the second segment.

The fourth chakra is connected to the thymus and related to green. The fourth segment, which is located in the thorax area, includes the following organs: heart, lungs, arteries, etc. The diaphragm is its demarcation with the abdominal part, while the upper part is demarcated by the shoulder muscles. It is in contact with the fifth segment only through the blood vessels that pass through the neck.

The fifth chakra is connected to the thyroid and related to blue. The fifth segment contains the parathyroid and is separated from the sixth segment by a strong diaphragm known as the tentorium, which separates the cerebellum from the brain.

The sixth chakra is connected to the hypophysis or the pituitary gland and related to violet. The sixth segment contains the brain and eyes and is separated from the seventh through the meninges.

The seventh chakra is connected to the pineal gland and related to purple.

Besides the diaphragms that separate the various segments, there are fibromuscular structures around the natural openings to prevent the loss of energy through these openings. Whenever these muscles weaken, they lead to an important loss of energy from the corresponding segment. In the lower part of the body, we find the anal sphincter, the urethral sphincter, and the vulvocavernous mucosa around the vaginal opening. Other muscles with these same functions are around the mouth and the eyes.

The presence of diaphragms (fibromuscular structures) among the various segments is a highly important factor. The fact that these fibromuscular diaphragms have high resistance and low energy permeability grants them a defensive function, which protects them against the negative influence of one segment on the other, something which might occur when there is an energy imbalance in a given segment. Imbalance is caused by a block in the center corresponding to the segment and is caused by a specific psychological conflict, as we shall see further on.

For example, whenever there is a territorial conflict causing the blocking of the first center, this influences the adrenal gland and other retroperitoneal tissues without causing damage to the adjacent sexual segment.

Further to the above-mentioned function of the fibromuscular diaphragms, other diaphragms protect against the loss of energy through natural openings. The pelvic diaphragm prevents the loss of energy from the urogenital segment to the outside, the urogenital diaphragm prevents the loss of energy through the urethra and the vagina, the anal sphincter prevents the loss of energy through the anus, and other sphincters have the same functions around other natural openings. For this reason, it is highly important to maintain the sphincter with a good muscular tone. The natural energy flow goes from outside toward the inside, and thus there is a continuous energy charge through the seven centers.

The Psychological Function
of the Seven Chakras

Energy centers are numbered according to their order and location in the body, starting from the lowest center—the first one, which is that of the coccyx until we reach the seventh, the highest one, which corresponds to the upper part of the head and is called the center of the corona.

All these chakras or energy centers are subdivided, in turn, into mental, emotional, anterior, and posterior, and each of them has two points of entrance—one anterior and one posterior—except the first center, which is single and is the energy entrance from down upward, and the center of the corona where the opposite direction is followed.

The second, third, and fourth chakras are, in their anterior part, emotional and receptive; through them, we can perceive all things around us, while in the posterior part, they are voluntary, giving us the force to act and convert our thoughts and emotions into action.

The center of the neck (5) and that of the forehead (6), which is also called the third eye, are both mentally sensitive, while in the rear they are mentally voluntary. The seventh center is merely mental.

When these three types of energy centers are in dynamic balance, the person enjoys good psychological and physical health. Therefore, in order to be balanced, the individual should have them all open, with a free entrance and exit flow and good rotating dynamism.

The base center receives low-frequency vital energy from the earth and determines the vitality of the physical body, while that of the corona receives high-frequency cosmic energy and determines the spiritual state of the person.

In general, the anterior mentally emotional centers cannot react with the external world if the corresponding posterior center is closed, because they would have no force of will to transform emotional intentions into actions, while when the anterior center is closed and the posterior opened, the person reacts without sentiments or reacts with rather negative feelings but without a dynamic movement of energy through the anterior center, thus causing behavioral and psychological disturbances.

Psychological conflict lead to a blockage of chakras that is a defensive reaction to protect against energy loss. Each chakra is related to a specific aspect in life, when we know which chakra is blocked, we know what psychological conflict the person has had. It is important to diagnose the energy center's blockage since we can diagnose and treat before psychological or physical symptoms appear.

When the anterior and posterior chakras are closed, they have no sentiments and have no force of will to act, and thus the individual will be apathetic and depressed.

The energy entrance through a given center contributes to the feeling of enjoyment. The larger the absorbed amount, the deeper the enjoyment sensation. Furthermore, enjoyment is specific to every center. The energy that enters through the first center gives us the pleasure of the material—a car, house, money, etc.—while the energy entering through the second center allows us to enjoy the pleasure of sex and so on and so forth for the other centers.

The energy flow can be transformed from inside toward the outside. When this happens, the individual loves. In fact, loving means giving. When an individual loves something or someone, he or she is capable of investing his or her energy in that thing or person. To love it or him or her means to provide energy to the beloved. The loved one enjoys this, because he or she receives energy and vitality. When the person is fully open and in harmony with nature, his or her energy status is good and should be capable of providing his or her energy without needing something in exchange for the love, which is unconditional love. However, it is always pleasurable to receive love.

Since there are seven energy centers and it is possible to love from each of them, we have seven types of love and seven types of pleasure.

The Seven Types of Love

We can define love as our capacity to give energy from within our system to the others. The energy flow can be manifested in the material aspect or remain as a pure energy the creates a sense of happiness. Since there are seven aspects in our life, there are seven kinds of love related to these aspects each one of them is related to one chakra and energy flow of love activates that segment and vitalize it. Therefore, the expectation to be loved in one of them creates the disappointment, delusion and suffer and blockage of the relating chakra. Here are the seven koinds of love:

- Material love: love of money, one's house, one's car, etc.—This love is perceived through the first center. Material love is love by which we give material things, such as money and gifts, especially things that we could need in our life. It is not a real material love when we give as a gift things that we do not need.
- Sexual love—love through which we express ourselves sexually, especially the males. In fact, the energy flow of the male during intercourse goes from inside toward the outside; it gives energy, while the female receives energy through sex giving sexual pleasure [enjoyment], and this happens because of the natural dynamics of energy during sexual contact. In man, energy comes from his sex, which he drags along during the ejaculation of the seminal liquid, while in the woman, energy comes from her chest toward the outside (sentimental love) and receives energy through the sex, enjoying the sexual pleasure. Thus,

we cannot ask for men to love like women, because men love through their sex and enjoy the pleasure of being sentimentally loved, while women love sentimentally and enjoy sex.

- Social love—this love comes through the third chakra, with which we link with individuals dear to us who are not our relatives. We love our friends, neighbors, the company, parties, etc.
- Sentimental love—this love comes from the chest and is divided into three classes:
  - maternal or paternal love for our parents and sometimes for our grandparents
  - fraternal love toward our brothers and sisters
  - sentimental love proper for our mate—This class of love, when it succeeds in involving all other centers, including the sexual one, becomes infatuation, which comprises a deep energy connection (psychological and spiritual) and a large energy flow through all centers. For this reason, it is said that a person in love is capable of giving his or her spirit to the loved one.
- Professional love, which is expressed through the throat
- Spiritual love—when the person starts to search beyond the physical world and finds special fascination in searching and experimenting in the spiritual world
- Divine love through which we get in contact with creative forces, the universal cosmic force, God

The Seven Types of Pleasure

Act for the present as if you would die tomorrow, and
for your future as if you would live forever.

—Arab proverb

We stated that receiving energy gives a feeling of pleasure; the type
depends on from which aspect of life we get the energy to be absorbed
by a given segment.

As there are seven types of love, there are also seven classes of pleasure.

1. Material pleasure—the individual enjoys increasing his or her
   material assets, winning the lottery, having a new and beautiful
   car, etc.
2. Sexual pleasure—when one receives sexual love
3. Social pleasure—the individual enjoys being accepted and loved
   by society
4. Sentimental pleasure—the pleasure of receiving sentimental
   love, of enjoying family love, of enjoying one's children, etc.
5. Professional pleasure—when one sees the results of one's work,
   which isn't but to get energy from one's work and enjoy one's
   work and one's self-expression.
6. Spiritual pleasure—many individuals meditate, sometimes
   day and night, because with this, they deeply enjoy receiving
   spiritual energy.

7. Divine pleasure, which takes place when one feels God's presence inside oneself, when one flows with the flow of nature, when one gets to be one with the eternal light—only then do we reach our true spiritual purpose, which all of us look for, whether consciously or unconsciously.

3. Intellectual Soul

Applying the universal energetic model described in the book *The Seven Principles and the Seventh Sense* clarifies the origin of the meridians described by the Chinese culture.

This results from the meeting between two poles—the positive and the negative. Each bipolar system has two poles, which are connected to each other by twenty-four meridians. Each two meridians are connected to one internal organ. The balance between the various organs having properties complementing each other is maintained by a continuous vital energy flow, which circulates along a "meridian" system on which are acupuncture stimulation points. Every time the flow between yin and yang is blocked, there appears an imbalance, which is expressed as disturbance or disease. Balance can be restored by inserting needles exactly in the stimulation points in order to restore the energy flow.

Each two branches in the spiral are identical in their direction of energetic flow and energetic frequency, and they are the source of that meridian from both sides of the body, for example, the left and right meridians of the lungs. The north pole, located in the thorax, has three spirals, each with four lines, thus creating twelve meridians that are connected through the fingers. The south pole, located in the pelvis, has twelve more meridians that end or start with the toes—a total of twenty-four meridians.

Where do these meridians originate, and how come there are twelve organs and twenty-four meridians?

I have found no mention in acupuncture books as regards their origin, but it seems to me that the energy structure model of quarks supplies a convincing explanation thereon.

In order to explain the connection between the energetic model and the meridians, we must return to the internal structure of the major poles.

As we have seen before in my book *The Seven Principles and the Seventh Sense*, each pole comprises three quarcones, each of which is made of four lines (quadrofila). The north pole in the thorax has three quarcones times four lines for each quarcone. We obtain twelve meridians that pass through the hands, and another twelve, linked to south pole, pass through the legs. Each two meridians are linked to one organ. From the thoracic pole, three descending negative lines originated, which are the heart meridian, the lung meridian, and the heart master. The other three positive ascending lines are the meridian of the small intestine, the large intestine meridian, and the triple heater. Ascending and descending meridians meet in the hands.

From the inferior pole, which is located in the abdomen, a further six meridians are originated: three negative ascending meridians, the kidney meridian, liver meridian, and pancreas meridian, and three positive descending ones, the bladder meridian, the stomach meridian, and the gall bladder meridian. These six meridians meet in the feet. One should be aware that in the superior pole, ascending lines are positive, while the descending ones are negative, and in turn, in the inferior pole, it is exactly the other way round (i.e., ascending meridians are negative, while descending meridians are positive).

Classical acupuncture with Chinese needles, whose roots go back to 2500 BCE, is the most ancient method of treatment known to us. At that time, Chinese treatment was only part of the religious-mystical philosophy that encompassed every area of life, starting from the recommended location of a house (known in art as feng shui) through to the suitable time in the year to sow the fields.

Traditional Chinese medicine views illness as an imbalance that can be examined according to eight patterns: interior/exterior, hot/cold, full/empty, yin/yang. The eight principles are an important basic paradigm in traditional Chinese medicine, as they show the location and nature of the imbalance. Using the eight principles, we learn the basic characteristics of the presenting imbalance.

The general theory of acupuncture is based on the premise that there are patterns of energy flow (chi) through the body that are essential for health. Disruptions of this flow are believed to be responsible for disease. Acupuncture may, it has been theorized, correct imbalances of flow at identifiable points close to the skin.

An acupuncturist practicing the classical Chinese method relates to illness as part of all the aspects related to the patient, the place where the treatment is given, the time of treatment, the day of the year, and even the date on which the person was born. After weighing all this data, the therapist tries to delicately balance the patient, using as few needles as possible and pricking a few but exact places. The treatment aims to discover the location of the imbalance in the body through diagnosis according to the pulse, the tongue, and the body, to strengthen that which is weak or scatter the strength if it causes energy to get blocked.

Results from a number of studies suggest that acupuncture may help ease types of pain that are often chronic, such as low-back pain, neck pain, and osteoarthritis/knee pain. It also may help reduce the frequency of tension headaches and prevent migraine headaches. Therefore, acupuncture appears to be a reasonable option for people with chronic pain to consider. However, clinical practice guidelines are inconsistent in recommendations about acupuncture.

Western doctors still think about the effects of acupuncture on the brain and body and neglect the real effect on the energy flow. This is the reason that how best to measure this effect is only beginning to be understood. Current evidence suggests that many factors—like expectation and belief—that are unrelated to acupuncture needling may play important roles in the beneficial effects of acupuncture on pain.

The upper part of the needles (see picture) is spiral, causing it to function like an antenna that connects the energetic line with the external field.

The treatments encourage the discharge of electrical surpluses from the body's energetic system, and the body is strengthened in cases of deficiency. This aids in recovering from illness and strengthens the human body to its maximum energetic potential. The treatment is suitable for most chronic problems from emotional problems through spinal problems, as well as for those suffering from back pain, muscle pain, and joint pain. A series of nine to eleven treatments are recommended to a patient in order to balance and maintain the body systems. Four more treatments annually are recommended during the transitional seasons for maintenance and prevention.

However, the use of acupuncture does not resolve the real cause that blocks the flow of energy in the meridian, which, as we will, is see related to emotional crises not elaborated and not expressed correctly. This, I believe, explains the limited results for some conditions.

The Study of Body Constitution

How the Energy of the Soul Influences the Constitution of the Body

From the medical point of view, the importance of the universal energetic model lies in the fact that it links energy and matter and explains the origin of structure and function (see *The Seven Universal Principles* book). The body structure is not random and is intended to maintain exact physiological functioning, as does the structure of the organs. The model enables us to understand the structural basis of the organ and explains the developmental process during life at two levels:

- the type of development of certain structures in the body, such as the facial structure, the body, the brain, and the heart, and their functional connection with the other systems;
- the structure of the seven systems in the body: the cardiovascular (veins and arteries and the lymphatic system), respiratory, digestive, nervous, reproductive, skeletal, and muscular

The duality of the body's structure and function and of the organs is similar to the duality existing in subnuclear particles—the wave and particle, two sides of the same coin.

Proper bodily functioning necessitates a proper structure of all the organs. Energetic change in the organ will lead eventually to structural change, and the physiopathological changes will become anatomical-pathological changes. Thus, for example, physical changes due to trauma can cause functional disturbances, such as acute myocardial infarction, and functional changes as a result of external disturbance (electromagnetic pollution) or internal disturbances (an energetic block as a result of emotional crises) will trigger physical changes (organic disease).

The universal energetic model blends medical knowledge from diverse sources and cultures into one mold and converts the mystical to scientific. It explains the source of the lines of force known in Chinese medicine as meridians, the source of the halo around the body, familiar in Indian medicine and other cultures, and the source and nature of the centers of energy known in Indian culture as chakras, and explain the difference between female and male energies and their manifestation in the body.

The differences between male and female energetic attributes are manifested in a person's behavior, regardless of his or her biological gender, since the quantity of male and female energy is connected to the love that we receive from our parents and the quantity of energy absorbed from the environment. Therefore, a man can have an excess of female energy and a woman can have an excess of male energy.

The male side is usually connected to our rationality, logic, linear thinking, and understanding. The female side is connected to feelings, nurturing, caring, compassion, love, and all the emotional qualities. Each of us has sides, the emotional and the mental. Very few people develop both equally; therefore, their cart often topples. Emotionalism is just as much a danger as thinking without being in touch with one's feelings. That too can go very much astray.

A person who goes too far on the side of rational thinking has to learn to balance with feelings, the female side. Anyone who thinks to the extent where the experience of feelings is hardly known has to practice much mindfulness of feelings. On the other hand, the female side is often emotionalism. This means we get carried away by our emotions and consequently our thinking is impaired. The quality of logical thinking, of delving into a thought process and being able to analyze, is not possible when the emotions are at the forefront.

The Characteristics of Male Energy

It is important to emphasize that we are speaking about energies and not genders. Each person, male or female, could have an excess of male or female energy or be in a balance state.

Male energy is characterized and represented in a strong, short, rigid, concentrated, contracted, closed, low, and heavy build. From the functional perspective, male energy is ascending, active, swift, transmitting, ongoing, impulsive, exact, warm, noisy, unstable, penetrating, light, separating, unorganized, impermanent, restrained, limited, crowded, linear, and logical, generating resistance to the environment, connected to the future.

A good example of the difference in behavior between the male and the female energy is found in the wild life of the humanbeing. A male that goes hunting is contracted, ready to attack the prey and to escape the danger, and therefore will concentrate on its goal and be disturbed by external stimuli. This situation has advantages and disadvantages. The disadvantages are connected to the contracted situation that results in restricting the reciprocal relations with the surroundings; the advantages are connected with withdrawal, which leads to greater resistance to external changes and therefore also to disease and epidemics.

Accordingly, the body build that represents those with excess male energy is contracted, rigid, thin, and strong-muscled, with a serious knitted facial expression that expresses concentration. The appetite of those with excess male energy varies, and sleep is usually more superficial.

From the psychological perspective, they are very sensitive, with strong genetic reactions, resulting in resistance to the environment, and can be reserved and introverted. However, they express themselves very well emotionally and mentally in their natural family environment. They are characterized to be jealous and conceited and are especially critical. They have a natural tendency to blame others and to emphasize the mistakes of others. When they talk, they use their index finger (or another object, such as a walking stick or pen) to point and poke others. They are very selective in their choice of friends and find it hard to love and make friends. This stems from mental rigidity and lack of ability to modify.

Intellectually, they are interested in knowing and their memory is selective (i.e., they concentrate on a relatively limited area and become experts therein). They tend to be deliberate, are logical, and measure everything according to rational criteria.

Emotionally, they are closed, especially in a nonfamily environment; they are frugal in emotional expression, do not like to shake hands, and certainly do not like to hug.

People with an excess of male energy have a need to buy things; they are parsimonious, quiet, and talk little, especially at work. Their faces hardly express emotions, and it is very rare to see them cry. Sometimes, they remain single or divorce easily. A small disappointment is enough for them to withdraw into themselves and to seek solitude. They are connected to work, sex and future.

The Characteristics of Female Energy

Female energy is typified by a broad build and by being soft, watery, and open. It goes from peripheral to central and is selfish, forward with descending movement, complex, big, heavy, and deep. Functionally, a person with female energy will be passive, light, calm, slow, nice, absorbing, conservative, traditional, unifying, connecting, constructive, organized, and connected to the past.

The female attributes can be compared to a female woman in the wild who likes to remain in her own territory and protect her children, who feels protected without the need to constantly be defensive and is sensitive to the outside surroundings. Her body build is weaker but has defenses.

Physically, female energy is manifested in a broad, roundish build, with thick but weak muscles and large bones. Her hair is usually thick and long; her face is full and round and covered with layers of flesh. Her cheeks and lips are full.

The physique of those with an excess of female energy is erect but not rigid. Their bodies are very sensitive and not resilient to the external environment; they can therefore suffer cold and heat, wounds, and be sensitive.

Psychologically, those with excess female energy are open to the external environment. They easily acclimatize to new surroundings, which helps their developmental process. At the same time, they become accustomed to their environment and sometimes find it hard to change it, which can cause a lack of psychological balance. They are characterized by protective motherly behavior. As children, they develop easily and at a uniform pace and reach emotional and mental maturity relatively quickly but remain connected to family places or to the country; they are traditional and find it hard to separate from their social group. Their psychological defense mechanism is weak, and therefore, they easily absorb outside influences.

Such people are open, tolerant, friendly, and generous and love company. They quickly adapt to change and are cordial to most people. They like to sing at home, in the street, and at work and are usually in a good mood. They always shake hands and hug happily. Those with excess female energy have weak self-control; they like to eat and drink, are connected to material things, and remain open to life's pleasures.

Intellectually, the openness to the external environment causes people with a surfeit of female energy to develop their external facet at the expense of their inner enrichment. They are realistic and sensual and need to see, feel, taste, and touch. In such a way, they learn reality directly without intellectual filters. They easily assimilate concrete things, such as numbers and names, and accept customs and social rules without reservation.

Those with excess female energy are not conceited; their self-esteem relies on the assessment of others. They are conservative and appreciate the status quo and are skilled and conversant with social rules and apply them. They cope with the situations in the manner convenient to them and thus ensure success. Their opinions are clear and practical, and they know how to apply the knowledge they have acquired, but they have fewer original ideas or new inventions.

They are open emotionally, friendly, and sensitive, and therefore, they smile and laugh easily but also cry readily. They cannot internalize their emotions and openly express happiness, sorrow, fear, depression, etc. Those with excess female energy are people who are suitable to family life and to social life, have many friends, and marry relatively early without careful choice of their partners. They are connected to home and to their mother and the past.

The Expression of the Balanced Build

People with balanced male and female energy enjoy vital dynamism affected by the dual movement of polar expansion and contraction. This build contains the physical and functional attributes of both the previous types—the male and the female.

People with balanced energy have high self-esteem; they know how to fuse the creative and revolutionary bents of male energy with the conservative female propensities. Their bodies combine both attributes and are therefore neither too expanded nor contracted but proportionately balanced. Such people embrace both the male and the female energy, opening up to them great potential in diverse realms.

It is important to remember that the quantity of male and female energy can be of diverse degrees in this type of build. Characterizing the energy is not restricted only to a polar situation of the male and female poles but is also affected by the elements—fire, air, water, and earth—that comprise the physical body (to be discussed later).

As noted, not every male necessarily behaves according to the attributes of his biological gender, since his physical, emotional, and sexual behavior is determined by the balance between the male energy and the female energy. The optimal formula is, of course, that which provides children with a balance of both types of energy. Thus, for example, an extreme and prominent shortage of male energy in a child, or shortage of female energy accompanied by a crisis of separation from the mother, can result in homosexuality. In contrast, an extreme shortage of female energy (lack of motherly love) or shortage of male energy, accompanied by a crisis of separation or sexual abuse from the father or other male, can cause lesbian tendencies. For all that, the physical presence of a father or mother still does not ensure balanced energy.

There are several essential conditions for receiving balanced energy:

- The parents must be physically and emotionally healthy to be capable of providing their children with love. Toys and presents cannot compensate for love.
- It is important to relate to a child's crisis seriously, to devote attention to him or her, and to help him or her reopen the channels of accepting love via the release of anger and tension.

A shortage of love and energy from both parents is likely to be manifested in the child in physical weakness, oversensitivity, allergies, and a tendency toward seclusion and depression. In a single-parent family, in which the mother raises the child alone, any other male figure (grandfather, uncle, or partner who is not the father) who provides the child with warmth and love can be sufficient to prevent an imbalance; this is also true when the father raises the child alone—any female figure who provides love can provide the child's female polar needs.

Four Energies of the Animal Soul

The physical body is a manifestation of the energies that guide and control its function. Each person has a particular energy that characterizes him or her and makes him or her a unique individual. These energies are described by different ancient cultures, such as Indian, Chinese, and Greek. Ayurveda in particular based its holistic medical system on the division of the persons according to their energy content. Ayurveda is a complete medical system that has been in use for more than five thousand years. It describes three fundamental universal energies, which regulate all natural processes on both the macrocosmic and microcosmic levels. That is, the same energies that produce effects in the various galaxies and star systems are operating at the physiology level. Ayurveda believes the five basic elements (space, air, fire, water, and earth) manifest in the human body as three basic humors, known as *tridoshas* (vata, pitta, and kapha).

- Pitta originates mainly from fire to which location is added; it is characterized by being keen, hot, and burning (fire).
- Vata originates in the air mainly but contains a very small amount of fire. It is characterized by being light, quick, cold, and dry.
- Kapha originates mainly in the earth and the water and is characterized by being heavy, slow, cold, and damp (water).

These three govern creation, maintenance, and destruction of bodily tissues as well as assimilation and elimination. Each person is born with a unique combination of these doshas, which determines their basic constitution, called prakruti. Understanding each person's prakruti is necessary for deciding which personal diet and exercise pattern, supplements and medicinal herbs, and cleansing and rebuilding therapies are right for him or her. This is among the chief methods, Ayurveda employs for the maintenance and restoration of health.

Ayurveda medicine recognizes the unique constitutional differences of all individuals and therefore recommends different regimens for different types of people. Although two people may appear to have the same outward symptoms, their energetic constitutions may be very different and therefore call for very different remedies. It focuses on establishing and maintaining the balance of the life energies within us, rather than focusing on individual symptoms. To balance the elements and the *doshas* of the body and the senses, there are many treatments, therapies, and exercises available. To balance the elements of the mind, meditations, mantra, and exercises are often used. Massage and *rasayana* treatments, along with visualization, *pranic* breathing, and other practices, allow personal access to intuition and the innate knowledge of the soul.

According to this method, two main means for attaining health and preventing or healing illness exist. The first is a lifestyle adapted to the laws of nature with an emphasis on correct nutrition, and the second is the use of medicinal herbs as food and medication, as well as massage oil, so that every person has an equal amount of dosha.

Ayurveda seeks to heal the fragmentation and disorder of the mind-body complex and restore wholeness and harmony to all people; therefore, the attending doctor checks the patient's pulse using special techniques and performs additional physical examinations should they be necessary. Thereafter, he or she talks at length with the patient to obtain a holistic image of his or her condition. All patients receive recommendations for food and lifestyle choices, and some of them receive additional recommendations, such as the use of simple and available medicinal herbs.

Although Ayurveda is considered be a holistic system, it does not take inconsideration the male-female trait differences and join water and earth humors in one dosha. Our model is systemic medicine too, dividing water from earth to have four humors instead of three; furthermore, we take into consideration the individual constitution that is a combination of the polarity of the major poles and the presence of one or more of the four elements. By doing so, as we will see, we divide the constitutions into sixty-four types that will be dealt with in detail in my book *The Human Code*. In this stage, I'll describe the characteristics of the four elements and their relation to the four physiological energies.

The Four Elements and the Four Physiological Energies

The human body is a perfect combination of material and energy. It is characterized by the presence of energy, whose source is in the animal soul, which revives it and enables its proper functioning in order to continue the perfection of the human soul. The magnetoelectric energy of the animal soul provides the vitality of the physical body and regulates the activity of parts of the body and the various organs.

The body is activated by four types of energy:

- biothermal energy
- bioelectronic energy
- biochemical energy
- biomechanical energy

The attributes of each of these energies are compatible with one of the four elements: biothermal energy with fire (heat), bioelectronic energy with air, biochemical energy with water, and biomechanical energy with earth.

The four types of energy are different expressions of the same energy, which experiences different stages that are compatible with the four stages of life. These four energies operate symbiotically within the cells and between the molecules and the atoms and ensure the proper functioning of the cells, the tissues, and, in fact, the entire body. Each of the four energies has a well-defined function; they are dependent in their functioning on each other in order to facilitate proper balance. Therefore, to enable this process, there must be a minimal amount of each type of energy in each cell.

The Basic Characteristics
of the Four Elements

Each one of the four elements is characterized by traits, aspects, and intensities that distinguish it from the other elements. All the elements exist in all the organs, but each of them is found in significantly greater concentrations in certain organs relative to others, causing the organ to be characterized by the dominant basic element. Every element is related to one of the four physiological energies and responsible for functional aspects of certain organs, as will be shown in the following sections.

Fire

Fire is characterized being stimulating, warm, light, dry, incisive, cutting, investigative, sharp, penetrating, alive, strong, rough, zesty, enlightening, clear, radiant, and pale, hence, its ability to alter things in a rising, melting, and penetrating manner.

Fire underlies every change in the organism, starting from digesting food in the stomach through sight to assimilating the sensory data in the brain.

In the body, the fire concentrates in the brain, the eyes, the liver, the spleen, the small intestine, the endocrine glands, the skin, the blood, and the perspiration.

The fire that is found in the enzymes and the gall bladder dissolves the enzyme, melts it, converts it to smaller particles, and prepares them for absorption. Therefore, a shortage of fire in the digestive system will make digesting food harder.

Fire is essential for changing and replacing the sensory data in our thoughts, for providing recognition, and for supervising the intellectual ability that enables comparison of two ideas in order to reach a conclusion.

When a person is free of blockages and the energy flows freely in his or her chakras and meridians, the fire enables it to react powerfully; if this energy is blocked and cannot find a natural outlet because of internal emotional crises or external environmental impacts, it can create anger, hatred, and jealousy.

Everything hot will increase the fire element in the body and can aggravate the lack of energetic balance. This increase can be connected to the quality of the food, behavior, geographic area, and climate.

The normal quantity of the fire element manifests balanced biothermal energy that facilitates proper digestion, good sight, a normal body temperature, radiant skin, intelligence, and clarity of thought.

- A lack of energy of fire can cause disturbances in the digestive system, deterioration in vision, a lack of light in the eyes, and a low body temperature to the point of feeling cold.
- An excess of the fire element leads to a feeling of heat and burning and to an increase in body heat, to overacidity that causes stomach indigestion, to a feeling of exaggerated hunger and thirst, and to a yellowish tinge to the skin.
- From the emotional aspect, an excess of the fire element can cause emotional confusion, anger, jealousy, fear, and a shortage of sleep; a lack of fire energy leads to a lack of physical strength and a decline in the joy of life, with judgmental and very critical behavior.

Fire and Biothermal Energy

Biothermal energy is the energy that warms and maintains the body's fixed temperature. The body heat is generated in the process of cellular breathing, during which energy is produced and is available for processes that demand it. The energy is produced by oxygenating organic material, such as glucose, fats, and proteins, occurring mainly in mitochondria. A chemical reaction can be the emission of energy, most of which is heat (about 70 percent) and part of which is intended for building ATP (see *The Seven Principles and the Seventh Sense*).

The quantity of heat produced by the body depends on the gender, body weight, quantity and quality of food, level of physical activity, and the outside temperature. The body temperature hardly changes due to temperature-regulating mechanisms that reduce dependency on the surrounding temperature. Animals and humans can therefore survive in extreme environmental conditions due to the regulation of the body's temperature through physiological, morphological, and behavioral mechanisms.

The body temperature is determined by weighing the metabolic rate, the effectiveness of converting energy to muscle work, the length of the physical exercise, the temperature of the environment, and the radiation. A rise in body temperature beyond the ideal temperature for its functioning activates the mechanisms to reduce the temperature. These include perspiration, transfer (the movement of heat from one part of the body to another part or to the external environment through touch), conduction, and radiation. These mechanisms depend on the internal factors that produce heat and on external factors, such as the environmental conditions (temperature, humidity, and wind speed).

The body's metabolic rate (BMR) depends on many aspects, the most important of which are the person's basic physique and his or her level of vitality. The metabolic rate is the rate of <u>energy</u> expenditure at rest, and is measured in kJ per hour per kg body mass. For example, a 55 year old woman weighing 130 lb (59 kg) and 5 feet 6 inches (168 cm) tall would have a body BMR of 1272 kcal per day or 53 kcal/h (61.3 watts).

The BMR and the amount of heat released from our bodies during eight hours of sleep varies from person to person, according to the four elements, but on average, it is 480 kkl. Every one gram of perspiration consumes 584 calories in evaporation, the source of whose energy is the body heat.

Since the various types produce heat and perspire differently, their objective body temperature and subjective feelings differ.

- People of the fire type produce a high temperature. The skin is hot and red even when they sleep. They perspire easily, and they sleep with an open window or with an air conditioner.
- People of the air type are thin, feel the cold, catch cold easily, must wear warm clothes even in the summer, and sleep fully covered wearing socks. Thus, it is possible to imagine the ongoing argument between couples when the man is of the fire type and the woman air. The man suffers from heat and wants to sleep with the window open or with an air conditioner, and the woman is cold and needs to cover herself and dress warmly.
- People of the water type produce regular or low heat, but the mechanism of lowering the heat (such as perspiration) is flawed as a result of the tendency to accumulate liquids. Therefore, such people suffer from heat, although their hands and feet can be cold and their skin temperature not high. Their physical activity is reduced since the body does not manage to lower the temperature efficiently.
- People of the earth type are cold when resting but produce considerable heat because of energetic physical activity. They perspire much and suffer from high temperatures.

The center that regulates heat is located in the hypothalamus, where it receives neural information from many sources, weighs it, and produces neural or hormonal reactions accordingly. In addition to regulating body temperature, this center is responsible for regulating water, salts, hunger, etc., which can be affected by the body temperature. Maintaining a stable body temperature is therefore very important.

Food and Biothermal Energy

Body heat can be provided by natural sources, such as the sun, and produced while oxygenating food or by artificial sources, such as hot cooked food or outside warming.

The energy produced by oxygenating food is measured in calories. The caloric density (the caloric value of each gram) of carbohydrates and proteins (about 4 kkl per gram) is far lower than the caloric value of fats (about 9 kkl per gram). Therefore, the production of heat in the process of cellular breathing is greater when burning fat than sugar. A drop in the temperature results in a hormonal reaction that increases the burning of brown fat, which is found in the bodies of babies under the age of one year and in the bodies of people who have adapted to severe cold. The color of this unique fatty tissue is the result of a very large quantity of mitochondria. A smaller quantity of energy is involved in the production of ATP in the mitochondria of the brown fat cell and in anaerobic breathing, and therefore, greater heat is released in this process.

Energy is derived from heat that is acquired in the process of cooking or from hot drinks and is measured in degrees.

Heat results from the nature of the food eaten. Paprika, for example, gives the feeling that it heats and even burns, even if its caloric value and temperature are not high. The sharpness feels like pain, caused by the stimulation and burning of the tiny nerve fibers of the taste buds. The material, which lacks smell or taste, in paprika, known as capsaicin, and the material known as piperine in black pepper are responsible for the burning feeling. Their impact on the body is similar to the impact of real heat, and they cause the brain to release endorphins, which are natural painkillers that increase the heart rate (intended to boost the metabolism), produce perspiration and saliva to freshen the mouth, and create a slight feeling of euphoria. These materials are known in biochemistry as catalysts, capable of considerably hastening the chemical reaction by reducing the energy necessary for activating them.

The Ayurvadic and Chinese approaches view the three types of energy as fire. This diagnosis is important for assessing a lack of integrative balance, manifested as a lack or an excess of the fire element among people and when the necessary food is recommended accordingly.

Healing by Heat

Body heat is regulated through a mechanism that considerably increases the flow of blood to the various organs by expanding the blood vessels. This process is possibly due to thermoreceptors that are scattered throughout the body; they constantly receive data regarding the body temperature and transfer it to the control center in the brain's hypothalamus. This is a sophisticated thermostat that processes all the information received, compares the data, and activates a range of possible reactions in order to stabilize the body temperature and enable proper functioning in a changing environment.

The change in temperature affects the speed of the chemical reactions, the spatial structure of the proteins and their activity, and consequently also the metabolic rate.

When the level of vitality is low, the rate of energy production in general and of heat in particular drop, thus affecting the metabolic rate. People then easily gain weight, although they do not eat a lot.

A drop in body heat below the thermal comfort range increases the metabolic rate and the production of heat, and consequently, the source of cell energy drops even more. Physical activity then further exacerbates the situation, since more blood flows to the muscles and the skin and less blood flows to the internal organs, such as the digestive system and the kidneys in order to allow the muscles to work and heat to be distributed. Hence, for people who are overweight as a result of the drop in the level of vitality, physical activity lowers that level and the metabolic level even further, resulting in overtiredness and a lack of weight loss. Exaggerated physical activity in such a situation has the result opposite to that desired.

When the body temperature drops below a certain threshold, shivering sets in, since in fact, the shaking of the muscles increases the production of heat and raises the metabolic rate (i.e., the rate of cellular breathing) by a factor of two or three.

The temperature is very important for the defense mechanism in fighting infections and inflammatory activity intended to correct damage to tissues. When bacteria or viruses enter the body, an infectious reaction develops, some of which is change in regulating the basal temperature in the hypothalamus. Consequently, mechanisms are activated that raise the production of heat in the cells and reduce its loss to the surroundings. This entire chain of reactions results in a rise in body temperature. At 39.3 degrees Celsius, bacteria find it hard to survive; a body temperature of 40 degrees Celsius awakens the immune system by activating the microphages, the T cells, the cytotoxic T cells, and the NK (natural killer) cells and lowers CD4-type cells.

Damage to the tissues, as after a heart attack or traumatic injury, causes an inflammation reaction and subsequently a rise in body temperature (above the thermal comfort range). This hastens the healing of the damaged tissue by increasing the blood flow to the infected area and increasing the metabolic rate in order to provide more energy for the healing process.

Therefore, it is important to respect the natural healing mechanism during which the body heat rises, rather than trying to lower the temperature unless it is very high (above 40 degrees) and the heat regulation mechanism does not function properly. A hot drink is recommended to help the body to continue regulating the proper heat in the presence of high temperatures, instead of cooling the body or taking a pill to lower the temperature. The blood vessels in the skin then expand and allow perspiration and movement and maintain the high and bearable temperature needed for the healing process.

The Use of the Sauna

The sauna is a wooden room that serves as a steam bath with damp or dry air at a very high temperature. It encourages excessive perspiration. In one corner of the room is a sauna stove, opposite which are built two or three stepped wooden bunks. The temperature varies between 80° and 100 °C (212 °F), higher on the upper platforms than on the lower platforms, so the users can choose the temperature they want. Such a high temperature is usually unbearable to the human body, and therefore, the level of humidity in the air is regulated to almost absolute dryness, making the sauna experience tolerable and even enjoyable. However, under many circumstances, temperatures approaching and exceeding 100 °C (212 °F) would be completely intolerable.

In the wet saunas, in which the level of humidity in the air can reach 100 percent, the temperature will be far lower than in the dry saunas. It will vary between 40 and 60 degrees Celsius. Despite the relatively low temperature in such saunas, the heat index from the combination of temperature and the degree of humidity is usually considered higher than that from dry saunas.

The immediate result of staying in the sauna is a rise in body temperature and increased activity of the mechanisms regulating body heat. This is manifested in the expansion of the blood vessels and overactivity of the sweat glands, processes that lead to a drop in blood pressure and in the supply of blood to the essential organs in the body. The body's reaction to these processes includes raising the breathing and pulse rates, as well as the excretion of adrenalin and endorphins. The impact of these is similar to the effect of morphine, offering a partial explanation for the pleasant feeling provided by the sauna.

Various studies have been published in recent years on the positive impact of the sauna, even, in contrast to common opinion, on cardio and cardiovascular patients.[43] Based on research, one may summarize the advantages and dangers of the sauna as follows:

Advantages

- a drop in blood pressure among patients suffering from high blood pressure[44]
- improved endothelial (inner layer) functioning of the arteries in patients at risk of heart disease[45]
- improved hemodynamic (dynamic blood flow) condition among patients with cardiac insufficiency
- improved lung functioning among patients with obstructive pulmonary disease[46-47]
- healing of the body's muscles and reduction of rheumatic pains in the muscles and joints[48]

Risks

- The use of the sauna under the influence of alcohol raises the risk of an extreme drop in blood pressure, fainting, and disturbance to the heart rhythm.
- Patients with severe aortic constriction, unstable angina pectoris, incidence of myocardial infarction a few days or weeks earlier, unbalanced cardiac insufficiency, and cardiac arrhythmia suffer the risk of a drop in blood pressure, fainting, repeated infarcts, and sudden death.
- A drop in blood pressure among patients receiving medication to lower blood pressure or with nitrates due to stable angina pectoris is also possible.

The extreme temperature in the sauna and the consequent increased perspiration are liable to cause rapid dehydration. Drinking a large quantity of water before and after sitting in the sauna is therefore recommended; spending more than fifteen minutes there is not recommended, and many saunas install an hourglass or other means of timing the stay there.

Hyperthermia

Hyperthermia (excessive heat) is a method of treatment that destroys growths and is the fourth method for treating cancer following operations, radiation, and chemotherapy. The use of hyperthermia in modern medicine started in the nineteenth century, when many doctors noticed that the cancerous growth shrank or even vanished among cancer patients who developed a high temperature due to the ongoing infectious disease. Coley's vaccine was developed by a doctor of that name, in which he infected a patient suffering from cancer with a virus that generated a high temperature and thus caused the shrinkage of the growths.

Hyperthermia is applied in hundreds of clinics and hospitals around the world and is included in the health basket in several European countries. It is based on a general rise in the body temperature that operates the immune system and on the focused absorption of energy within the growth tissue. Two levels of temperature affect cancerous growths through the various hyperthermic mechanisms:

- a high to extreme temperature that is insufficient for directly destroying the cells
- a very extreme temperature that causes changes in the structure and the direct destruction of the cells.

There is no consensus as to what is the safest or most effective target temperature for the whole body. During treatment the body temperature reaches a level between 39.5 and 40.5 °C (103.1 and 104.9 °F).

Wolf, Peter (2008). *Innovations in biological cancer therapy, a guide for patients and their relatives.* Hannover: Naturasanitas. pp. 31–3.

However, other researchers define hyperthermia between 41.8–42 °C (107.2–107.6 °F) (Europe, USA) to near 43–44 °C (109–111 °F) (Japan, Russia).

"Hyperthermia in Cancer Treatment: A Primer". Medical Intelligence Unit. 2006.

Two main events occur in cases of high to extreme temperatures (of up to 40 degrees Celsius). The blood vessels expand immediately when the tissue absorbs high heat, and thus the blood flow to areas is warmed and the supply of nutrients increases. The metabolic processes are accelerated, and the quantity of energy available to the ATP cells rises. Consequently, cell division ceases.

In reaction to the heat, the growth cells produce heat shock proteins, located on the cell envelope, to protect them from the next blast of heat. The immune system identifies these proteins as "foreign" to the body and dispatches the cells of the immune system to attack and destroy them. This mechanism explains the effect of the thermal energy even if it does not manage to directly destroy the cells. In contrast, at very extreme temperatures, the heat directly destroys the cancerous cells by either denaturing (destroying) the proteins as a result of which there are changes in the cell skeleton and in the membranes, damaging the enzymes and other components of the cell that are important for the synthesis and correction of the DNA (the process of fixing the damage demands considerable energy that is not available in the cancerous cells, while the normal tissue has a more effective and more rapid system for correcting damage); or by causing edema around the growth tissue, making it hard for the blood to flow freely to the area.

The contraction of the blood vessels in the growth tissue under the impact of the heat denies the supply of nutrients and oxygen to the growth cells for an extended period of time, thereby damaging their ability to grow and develop.

This type of hyperthermia occurs in localized treatment together with chemotherapy or radiation. The method is undergoing clinical testing at several treatment centers in Israel and globally with encouraging results.

Studies that explored the treatment of cancerous growths using methods that combine hyperthermia with radiation and hyperthermia with chemotherapy show a slightly higher rate of growth shrinkage and a slightly longer survival time compared to treatment with each method separately. For example, published studies have shown an improvement of 10 year disease free survival in bladder cancer patients treated with combined hyperthermia and chemotherapy- 53% survival, versus those treated with chemotherapy alone, 15% survival after 10 years.

Colombo R, Salonia A, Leib Z, Pavone-Macaluso M, Engelstein D (March 2011). "Long-term outcomes of a randomized controlled trial comparing thermochemotherapy with mitomycin-C alone as adjuvant treatment for non-muscle-invasive bladder cancer (NMIBC)". *BJU International* **107** (6): 912–8.

Whole-body hyperthermia has also been found to be helpful for depression.

Hanusch KU, Janssen CH, Billheimer D, *et al.* (July 2013). "Whole-body hyperthermia for the treatment of major depression: associations with thermoregulatory cooling". *The American Journal of Psychiatry* **170** (7): 802–4.

Air Element

The air energy sets everything into motion in the body and the psyche, and it is, therefore, considered the cause of all movement, starting from the smallest physical molecule through to thought.

Air has the following properties: it is light, active, swift, mobile, changing and changeable, dry, cool, thin, and rough. Its ethereal trait provides a clear picture—empty, self-understood, transparent, dry, contracted, excited, spoiled, unstable, irregular, eccentric, spasmodic, scattered, evaporating, and unorganized.

Since air tends to be dry, everything dry that penetrates the body will amplify this element.

The air is concentrated in the brain, the nervous system, the heart, the lungs, the large intestine, the skin, the bladder, the pelvis, the bones, the muscles, and the ears. It enters the body through breathing and through the skin; a change for the worse in the air or its excess in the body is excreted by exhalation and with the gas from the large intestine.

Air is important for the movement of food in the digestive system; an excess or shortage can increase or inhibit this. Air therein is mainly in the stomach and the small intestine; it assists the digestive process as it helps the excretion of digestive juices and the stomach movements. An excess or lack of air will upset the balance between water and the digestive juices.

The role of air in the brain is important in the process of creating memory. It provides a dynamic of thought through its storage in the memory archive, retrieving thought from the unconscious to the conscious and its return again to the memory archive.

A normal quantity of air in the body is manifested as balanced electromagnetic energy that provides a feeling of lightness of movement, speed of thought, and strong intuition.

- An excess of air will led to a decline in physical strength, exaggerated loss of weight, diarrhea, insomnia, shaking, nervous ticks, dizziness, and weakness of the immune, the sensory, and the motor systems, as well as deformities in embryos and a variety of pains.
- A shortage of air will result in a decline in all physical and emotional activity, digestive disturbances, nausea, pain, feelings of discomfort, loss of the sense of smell, and depression.
- Emotionally, an excess of air will cause emotional and sensory disturbances, fear and anxiety, hallucinations, and disruption in daily functioning.

Bioelectronics Energy

Bioelectronics is a recently coined term for a field of research that works to establish a synergy between <u>electronics</u> and <u>biology</u>.

<u>"A Framework for Bioelectronics: Discovery and Innovation"</u>. National Institute of Standards and Technology.

Every living creature has an electromagnetic field created by biochemical and mechanical activity.

All the cells in our bodies are characterized by the basic electrical activity that allows the essential activity typical of living cells. The internal (in tissue and cells) and the external electromagnetic forces are very important for maintaining harmony in our health.

The geomagnetic field outside our bodies, originating in the globe's polar force, affects the physiology of the organs. The earth's rotation around the sun causes seasonal changes, and the daily cycle of light and dark affects the immunoneuroendocrine system with implications for feelings and emotions.

Electrical activity in the cell also exists in a state of rest, as a result of a different drop in the level of ions beyond the cell membrane. Thus, for example, there is a low concentration of sodium ions and a high concentration of potassium ions in the cytoplasm (cellular fluid) compared to concentrations outside the cell. As a result, an electrical fall is created, known as the rest potential. This stable situation is feasible because of the activity of the ATPase-NaK enzyme, which consumes more than a quarter of the energy (ATP) of the metabolic activity of a regular cell. This enzyme operates the channels of the membrane and preserves the different concentrations of the diverse ions that create the electrical fall and is under the influence of the magnetoelectric field.

The energetic transfer between two magnetic poles causes the appearance of the four stages of life, with a change in the magnetic moment that activates the ATPase-NaK enzyme. The magnetic field thus controls the cell's electric field. A deviation in the cell's electric potential can cause significant changes in the chemical reactions and in the genetic manifestation of the DNA, which can affect protein synthesis and new biological activity and even alter our behavior. The electrical activity in the nervous system causes changes in the infiltration of materials to the synapses (points of connection between the nerve cells) and the excretion of a nerve conductor or neurotransmitter (a molecule that moves between one nerve cell and another). These generate changes in arousal in the adjacent cell and alter the electrical activity, resulting in the excretion of hormones into the blood, which reach the target cell (known as the postsynaptic cell). They alter the electrical condition therein, as well as in the striated muscle, the smooth muscle, and the heart muscle, and thus generate muscle contraction. The rest potential depends on the cell's level of vitality. With the weakening of the cell's magnetic field, the rest potential drops as does the level of arousal. There is also a decline in biochemical energy, which creates the ATP, resulting in a decline in electrical activity due to disturbance to the ATPase-NaK enzyme functioning.

Familiarity with the bioelectric nature and understanding of how the electrical activity created from the physical, emotional, and spiritual activity affects and integrates with the external environment are therefore very important.

The strength of the polar force in organs can be measured through the cell's rest potential. This index expresses the difference in electrical potential between the cytoplasm and the extracellular space. The electrical activity of the various organs is useful in diagnosis. The instruments measure their spontaneous electrical activity and their electrical activity in reaction to electrical and nonelectrical stimuli.

Tools for Measuring Spontaneous Electrical Activity

- ECG—electrocardiograph, developed in 1887 to measure the heart's electrical activity
- EEG—electroencephalograph, developed in 1875 to measure the electrical activity of various areas of the brain
- Chinese electric pulse testing—the Chinese method of examining the electricity of the pulse. For thousands of years, the Chinese used the pulse as an index of the various health conditions. Technology was developed in recent years to measure the electrical changes in the various types of pulse.
- Electogastrointestinalograph (Chinese gastrointestinal analysis)—the EGEG is a tool developed recently in China to detect the electrical activity of various areas in the digestive system, similar to an ECG, where different types of electrical activity were identified as associated with illness in the digestive system. The developers of this method emphasize its advantages over invasive methods, such as gastroscopy or colonoscopy (examination of the large intestine) or the use of barium and imaging using laser rays. This method enables identification of certain stomach ulcers, cancerous growths in the stomach, a spastic colon, or an inflammation in the pancreas using noninvasive methods.

Tests that Measure Secondary Electrical Activity to Nonelectric Stimuli

- Cardiac stress test or ergometry—ECG notation under gradually increasing effort in order to identify disturbances in the flow of blood in the coronary arteries and to predict heart disease
- Sleeping or sleep-deprivation electroencephalogram—can discover situations that cannot be diagnosed through a regular EEG
- Nystagmometry—the use of hot or cold water to measure the movement of the eyes in reaction to stimulation of the ears to identify problems in the middle ear
- Electrical reaction in the skin—measuring the electrical conductivity between two points on the skin, similar to a polygraph that measures the sympathetic reaction to diverse stimuli that cause perspiration and alter conduction. This tool, intended to teach the patient to lower the level of stress, is used in biofeedback technology.

Tests that Measure Secondary Reactions to Electromagnetic Stimuli:

- Electromyograph—the electrical stimulus of the nerve and the reaction of the muscle provide important information on the functional condition of the muscle or the nerves connected to it
- Brain stem audiometry—the patient is exposed to sound at various frequencies, and the brain waves that react to stimuli are measured in order to explore the source of disturbances to hearing
- Cochlear microphonics—a sensitive electrical instrument is placed in the cochlea in the inner ear and measures the electrical activity in reaction to sounds at differing frequencies in order to assess cochlear functioning
- X-rays—electromagnetic energy that is radiated through the body and received on the other side; it reflects the condition of the various tissues that absorb this energy differently and is used to diagnose the presence of pathological tissue
- Magnetic resonance imaging (MRI)—the body is exposed to a strong magnetic field, whose reflection is characterized by five variables that enable differentiating between the various tissues that appear as pictures
- Ultrasound—an echograph that uses supersonic waves, which are received differently by the different tissues and facilitates distinguishing between fatty tissue, fluid tissue, and bones. It is in extensive use to diagnose the condition of the heart muscle

and the valves, to examine the stomach cavity and the breasts
to discover growths or cysts, and to examine the kidneys and
brain

- Binocular iriscorder—measures the reaction of the iris to
the exposure to electromagnetic energy in the form of light.
It enables attaining important information on the activity
of the optic nerve, on the autonomous nervous system, and
on diagnosing pesticide poisoning or damage to the nervous
system.

- **Bioelectrical impedance analysis** (BIA) is a commonly used
method for estimating body composition, and in particular
body fat. The impedance measurement is generally measured
from the wrist to the contralateral ankle and uses either two or
four electrodes. A small current on the order of 1-10 uA is passed
between two electrodes, and the voltage is measured between
the same (for a two electrode configuration) or between the
other two electrodes.

- Am J Clin Nutr-1996- Keneth R Foster and Henry C Lukaski

- From the BIA the phase angle can be measured. Phase angle is
a linear method of measuring the relationship between electric
resistance (R) and reactance (R_c) in series or parallel circuits.
Taking the arc tangent value of the ratio of reactance versus
electric resistance provides us with the phase angle value.
Lower phase angles appear to be consistent with low reactance
and equals either cell death or a breakdown in the selective
permeability of the cell membrane. There is a significant
difference in phase angle between healthy and disease states.
The phase angle increases with improving clinical status.

Kushner RF. Bioelectrical impedance analysis: A review of principles
and applications. J Am Coll Nutr.1992;11:199–209.

Foster KR, Lukaski HC. Whole body impedance- what does it
measure? Am J Clin Nutr. 1996;64:388–396.

Water Element

The main purpose of water is to lubricate, moisten, maintain flexibility, and be fatty, slippery, sticky, soft, comfortable, protected, accepting, and penetrating. Water enters the body through the liquids that we drink and the moist food we eat. The use of water enables preserving a suitable surrounding for all the biochemical and physiological processes that occur in watery solutions.

Water is characterized by being cold, liquid, and soft. The liquidity enables it to flow downward without a defined shape of its own.

The water in the body is concentrated in the brain, the synovial fluid, the lubricating fluid in the joints, the seminal fluid, the kidneys, the bladder, the tear and saliva glands, the mouth, the stomach, the lymph fluids, the neck, fats, the pleura and the pericardium, the peritoneal cavity, and the spinal cord fluid. All liquid material that penetrates the body increases the water element.

A normal quantity of the water element allows a good biochemical reaction in the tissues and proper activity of the joints by lubricating them and maintaining their flexibility and that of the pleura, the peritoneum, and the meninges and proper secretion from the mucus tissue in order to protect and provide softness to the body and distribute heat. From the perspective of the soul, proper functioning leads to tolerance and easy adaptation to changing situations and flowing with events and the life process.

Excess water will lead to the accumulation of liquids in the peritoneum and the pericardium that is manifested in discharges—the accumulation of liquids in the stomach cavity in the form of stomach discharges, edema in the lower limbs, the accumulation of liquids throughout the body, and a rise in weight.

The lack of water will cause rigidity in the connecting tissues, deficiency in the sense of taste, and dryness of the skin or of the membranes mentioned previously, physical pain, rapid heart rate, and insomnia.

Biochemical Energy

Biochemistry is one of the secondary sciences of biology and deals with biological molecular activity (sugars, proteins, fats, and nucleotides) and the reciprocal activities between them. Biochemical activity is possible because of the reduction-oxidation (redox) process in environmental conditions with certain basic acidity.

Redox is a common and basic reaction. Reduction and oxidation are two reactions that occur simultaneously, when one material is reduced and the other oxidized. A reducer is a material that provides electrons; an oxidizer receives them. Whatever transfers electrons undergoes oxidation (i.e., the oxidizer undergoes reduction) and the reducer undergoes oxidation.

A common oxidation reaction is the burning or decomposition of the sugars in the body. This process affords the source of the biochemical energy and starts the decomposition of the nutrients (glucose, protein, or fats) with oxygen. After a lengthy and complex process, the electrons pass from reduction to oxidation, releasing CO_2.

The entire process allows the conversion of food to energy in the form of ATP, which is needed for all cellular activity, in the course of which many enzymes hasten the processes by reducing or oxidzing other materials. The electrons that are released while decomposing the glucose are absorbed by the two electron carriers NAD (nicotinamide adenine dinucleotide) and FAD (flavin adenine denucleotide). The NAD is a very important organic compound for all living creatures and functions in the cell as an electron carrier; it is capable of absorbing a hydrogen ion comprising two electrons and a proton, with a known negative ion hydrogen (H) and transferring them to another compound. This process enables many chemical reactions in the cell, and too many life processes to count would not exist without NAD.

The main source of energy in the body is obtained from glycolysis or from glucose decomposition, which can occur in the presence of oxygen as an aerobic process or without oxygen as an anaerobic process.

Glycolysis starts with the cytoplasm of the cell without needing oxygen; the glycolysis that contains six atoms of carbon undergoes a series of ten chemical reactions, at the end of which it is factorized into two molecules of pyruvate, each of which contains three carbon atoms.

The energy derived in the glycolysis process is in the form of ATP molecules—known as the "energetic coin" of all living creatures. During glycolysis, two ATP molecules are consumed and four are formed (i.e., the energetic gain is two ATP molecules).

Three products result from this process—two ATP molecules, two hydrogen-carrying molecules known as NADH, and two molecules of pyruvic acid.

The anaerobic process also occurs in our muscle cells when they function with maximum effort. No additional ATP molecules are created in this process, and therefore, the final energetic profit of the process of converting the pyruvic acid to lactic acid is only two ATP molecules (the two molecules obtained at the first stage, the glycolysis stage).

The aerobic process occurs in mitochondria in the presence of oxygen. The pyruvate is converted to acetyl coenzyme A, which affords the start of a Krebs cycle, at the end of which the acetyl coenzyme decomposes into CO_2 and water.

Only two molecules of ATP are formed in the anaerobic glycolysis process, and thirty-six molecules in the process of the disintegration of the pyruvic acid into carbon dioxide and water. Hence aerobic breathing entails thirty-eight molecules of ATP.

The Krebs cycle affords a metabolic junction of supreme importance. All the intermediate products of the cycle synthesize and develop diverse materials in the cell (anabolism). In addition, many compounds that we use in food and from which energy is not derived directly (nucleotides, fatty acids, and amino acids) disintegrate in the cell and their products are converted to intermediate products of the Krebs cycle, so that they can enter the cycle directly and feed it.

The cellular breathing process entails three stages:

- The glycolysis process produces pyruvate, which is converted to acetyl coenzyme A and enters the Krebs cycle at stage 2.
- Stage 2 occurs in mitochondria and is termed the Krebs cycle. Its product is two recurring coenzymes, NAD and FAD (bearing excess electrons). The electrons originate in acetyl coenzyme A, which disintegrates at stage 1.
- Stage 3 is NAD and FAD, donate them to oxygen at the end of the cellular breathing process.
- The movement of the electrons from the food (starting with the cellular breathing process) to the oxygen (the end of the process) is accompanied by the expression of energy needed to create ATP, which the cell is capable of using at a later stage.

Free Radicals

Chemically, a free radical is an atom that has a single unbalanced electron in its external envelope. Such an electron protests the stability of the material. If the atom is part of the molecule, then the entire molecule is a free radical. Free radicals are not stable but are very active chemically (i.e., they react with the diverse materials found in their environment). Furthermore, they can steal electrons from another essential molecule and consequently disrupt proper functioning; in turn, they become free radicals, generating a chain of undesirable chemical reactions.[49]

The most common free radical is oxygen, whether as an isolated atom or as part of a molecule. Studies show that 2 to 5 percent of the oxygen we inhale (whether when at rest or under physical exertion) can become free radicals. At the same time, the claim that a larger quantity of free radicals is created during physical activity, when a large quantity of oxygen is inhaled, is simply incorrect. We have seen that oxygen does not affect life expectancy, cause early aging, or produce free radicals in animals for whom physical activity is an effort and who inhale a large quantity of oxygen. Examples of this are the bat, whose life expectancy is thirty years, ten to fifteen times that of the mouse; most fowl live long lives relative to their heart rate, with the Australian parrot living some fifteen years.

The greater the progress in molecular research of the illnesses, the more illnesses caused by an excess of free radicals are discovered. Some claim that they contribute to the development of sixty different illnesses and conditions in the human body, including the atrophy of the mitochondria of the brain cells and the development of Alzheimer's and Parkinson's, heart disease, cancerous growths, and wrinkles. Thus, for example, the cell membrane that contains many fatty acids is harmed by the activity of the free radicals. The cells' ability to absorb nutrients and remove waste is then affected, leading to destruction of the cell. The free radicals also cause damage to the hereditary material, to the point of change in the structure of the DNA and the RNA and the appearance of cancerous growths.

With aging, there is a decline in the level of cell vitality and a rise in the number of free radicals. Cross-matches are performed between the chain of the various proteins that alter the proteins and damage their functioning, causing a drop in the functioning of the antibodies and a disturbance in transporting materials in the body and in various reactions that are hastened by enzymes (made of proteins). The cross-matches are also responsible for changes in the skin and the appearance of wrinkles as they affect the collagen and elastin that afford the skin its strength and flexibility.

A certain quantity of free radicals is essential and fulfills vital functions in the body, such as absorbing bacteria and creating connections between the collagen fibers in the skin. In a vital and balanced body, antioxidant enzymes exist to neutralize the free radicals and prevent them from harming the body. The neutralizing mechanism functions in such a way that antioxidants contribute an electron to the free radical molecule, without themselves becoming free radicals, and thus they halt the chain process of stealing electrons. In frequent strenuous physical activity, a larger quantity of free radicals is generated as the consumption of ATP increases. These can damage the muscle tissue, attack the proteins, and oxygenize fats in the body and convert them into free radicals too.

Many factors hasten the creation of free radicals, including fried food, smoking, medication, sprays and disinfectants, air pollution, radiation, and cleaning materials. They affect the body's ability to protect itself from free radicals that are created naturally. And indeed, if there is an excess of free radicals in the body and insufficient decomposing enzymes, as there are at a mature age, the damage of the free radicals increases and they afford the main reason for accelerated aging.

Protection from the Free Radicals

Too low levels of antioxidant vitamins (vitamins A, C, and E) can increase the risk of several chronic diseases. Since most people do not use the optimal quantity of all the vitamins with their meals,[50] we recommend adding foods and food additives to the diet that help to fight the free radicals. Thus, for example, proper consumption of vegetable and fruit juices neutralizes the free radicals and prevents damage to the tissues and cells. We further recommend adding vitamins, such as vitamin C, beta-carotene, quo-enzyme, lipid Q10 alpha acid, licopan, vitamin E, selenium, and zinc whose effectiveness has been scientifically proven. Potassium can also be combined with vitamin C in the form of potassium ascorbate, and the antioxidizing ability of the two components can be explored.

In addition to nutrition, moderate physical activity and lowering stress are important for protection from the impact of free radicals.

Alkalinity and Acidity

The chemical reactions within the cell are facilitated and regulated by the level of acidity of the solution, which is measured as pH, itself determined according to concentrations of hydronium ions (H_3O^+) in the solution. This concentration is measured in moles per liter. P represents the potency (i.e., its concentration) and H represents positive hydrogen ions (protons, H^+).

The value pH = 7 refers to the level of acidity of distilled water in which the concentration of H+ ions is equal to the OH^- concentration (neutral solution pH = 7). If a compound is added to the water that contains hydroxide ions, and if the values of pH are higher than 7 with the concentration of H^+ lower than the concentration OH^-, the solution will become basic. If acid is added to the water that contains hydrogen ions, it will disintegrate, and the result will be pH values lower than 7, including an H^+ concentration that is greater than the OH^- concentration. In this case, the solution is acidic.

The normal range of the pH scale is 0 to 14, embracing most of the solutions in nature. As mentioned, pH = 7 indicates neutral acidity. Values greater than 7 indicate an alkaline situation, while values lower than 7 indicate acidity.

Physical health is directly dependent on a balance in the level of acidity in the blood. Each cell in the body functions optimally in a certain range of pH. Thus, for example, the pH of the stomach is 1 to 3, of the urine 4.5 to 8, of the skin 4.5 to 7, of saliva 6 to 7.4; of pancreatic excretion 8 to 8.3; of blood, it is in the narrow range of 7.35 to 7.45. A slight deviation from this range can lead to a disturbance in the functioning of the organs. Therefore, the balance between acid and base is one of the important dimensions of health.

Some people suffer a significant deviation from the proper pH range, manifesting itself in metabolic acidity. This is considered a serious medical problem, which appears after renal insufficiency or after an intestinal operation that causes a loss of basic solutions. These cases are at a very high level of risk, which necessitates close monitoring, and the patients are usually hospitalized in intensive care units.

In contrast, many live with low-grade metabolic acidosis resulting from the quality of modern nutrition since most food is extremely acidic, leading to a high level of acidity. Low-grade metabolic acidosis does not enjoy any attention from the medical establishment, despite its great importance and the accumulated scientific evidence indicating the direct connection to the development of atrophic illnesses through to cancerous growths. This is a situation of chronic acid stress and a common factor for many illnesses that affect the bones, joints, nervous system, intestine, and kidneys.

When food is consumed, digested, and absorbed, each of its components can generate an acidic or basic reaction in the blood and the kidneys. The average nutrition today is 50 percent more acidic than previously, and the diet has a very high acidic load compared to a diet that used to be more basic.[51]

The exchange of foods producing basicity for foods generating acidosis is mainly the result of replacing fruit and vegetables with cereal-rich, energy-full foods that are rich in animal protein, processed, and poor in vitality.

In general, some 20 percent of our nutrition today is basic and 80 percent of it is acidic. Frassetto et al. show that modern acidic nutrition generates low-level metabolic acidity. Thus, much of the population is at high risk of metabolic acidity.[52]

Studies find that as long as the activity of the lungs, kidneys, heart, skin, and the entire body declines, so the level of acidosis in the blood, saliva, and urine increases.[53,54,55] Thus, osteoporosis, illnesses related to hormones decline, and the loss of muscle mass at a more advanced age can also be the result of low-grade metabolic acidosis. In fact, overacidosis exists in all the degenerative illnesses, such as cancer, heart disease, osteoporosis, rheumatism, gall bladder and kidney stones, damage to the immune system, *Candida* (overdevelopment of yeast fungi), plaque, acne, cold hands and feet, muscle pains, and a lack of energy. Chronic acidity can also cause a drop in IGF-1 activity (i.e., in growth factors that are also known as IGF [insulin-like growth factor] or somatomedins).[56,57,58] One can develop resistance to the growth hormone (GH resistance),[59,60,61] a drop in the functioning of the thyroid and hypothyroidism,[62,63] and the exaggerated secretion of cortisol (hypercortisolemia).[64,65,66,67,68]

The body has mechanisms intended to maintain a balanced pH level. Thus, for example, in the case of excess acidity as a result of eating acidic food, the acidity needs to be neutralized through a mechanism that creates a base. However, overuse of the balance mechanisms is liable to cause an organic lack of balance, functional disturbance, and physical illness.

The balance mechanism, the homeostasis, enables maintaining the pH in the blood at a level of 7.4. This process functions through the excretion and sedimentation of acidic and basic minerals from various parts of the body, such as the bones, the soft tissues, body fluids, and saliva. Therefore, there can be tremendous changes in the pH of these tissues.

In a healthy situation, the pH in the blood, of the spinal fluid, and of saliva is 7.4; hence, the pH of saliva is parallel to the acidity of the extracellular fluid and therefore reflects the balance and acidity in the body. The pH of saliva among healthy women varies from 7.1 to 7.5; a pH of 6.5 indicates slight acidity, while 4.5 indicates serious acidity. The pH of saliva among most children is 7.5, while for 50 percent of adults, it is found to be lower than 6.5, testifying to the decline in the level of vitality, lack of calcium, and a low quality of life. For terminal cancer patients, pH values of saliva are about 4.5.[69]

There are several mechanisms for stabilizing pH values to the optimal levels.

Releasing calcium from the bones—Calcium is a strong base that can neutralize the exaggerated level of acidity. The source of calcium for this purpose is bone, which contains the richest pool of calcium in the body. Chronic low-grade metabolic acidosis causes the release of calcium from the bone, which is transferred to the urine and is released with the acid it neutralized. Therefore, if the nutrition is acidic over time, a negative calcium balance will develop, the bones will weaken, and osteoporosis will result.[70,71,72,73,74,75] The chronic acidity can be neutralized by eating fruit and vegetables, especially those that produce the most basic reaction (spinach, celery, carrots, etc.), which many doctors and specialists now understand to be the most effective way of improving bone health.[76]

2. A negative nitrogen balance (a high concentration of nitrogen in the urine): excreting ammonia (NH_4) from the kidneys is an effective way to neutralize acids in the blood. Most of the nitrogen in ammonia comes from glutamine, which is the strongest basic amino acid, more frequent than all the amino acids of the proteins that build the muscle. Since the muscle cells contain the richest pool of glutamine, metabolic acidity causes disintegration of the muscle (in order to release glutamine from it). In the kidneys, this glutamine undergoes enzymatic

decomposition, as a result of which the anabolic activity (construction) and the protein synthesis weaken, the muscle loses protein, and negative balances of nitrogen and protein result.[77]

3. Potassium and magnesium (in addition to calcium) are also means of neutralizing the excess acid in the body. These minerals are found in vegetables and fruits, and therefore, they provide a basic reaction for the body.

In the healing process, it is important to examine the balance of the basic acids and to correct the deviations by the use of suitable foods and the addition of minerals and meditation.

Measuring Biochemical Energy

The body's biochemical energy is the foundation for maintaining the basic activities of all the cells and tissues and affords a biological basis for all the body's essential activities. Thus assessment of the biological condition provides us with a basis for understanding the body's energetic condition and allows us to correct divergences prior to the appearance of physical illnesses. The concept of the biological terrain is attributed to the physiologist Claude Bernard of the nineteenth century. He believed the functioning and wholeness of the cell is determined by its surroundings, chemical foundations, amino acids, enzymes, and electrons.

In 1935, the French hydrologist Louie-Claud Vincent developed the first instrument for examining the biological terrain. In 1950, he reached the conclusion that the key to understanding corporal health lies in measuring and diagnosing the basic elements found in the body fluids: blood, urine, and saliva. In 1962, he defined anew the three most important factors for determining the biological ground:

- pH, which measures the basic-acid balance
- rH, which measures the level of free ions and expresses the oxidation-reduction condition
- R, which represents electrical resistance, indicating to the level of minerals

The new version of this test is known as the biology terrain assessment (BTA). It is conducted using a mobile appliance that samples 2 cm³ of body fluid (saliva, urine, blood) after a twelve-hour fast.

The various parameters are analyzed electronically and fed into a computer, which provides an exact mapping of all the parameters within a few minutes. The computer simultaneously analyzes the results, indicates the systems that should be treated, and suggests ways of handling it.

Defining the basic-acid (pH) and RedOx of the patient's metabolism is important in diagnosis or treatment to avoid exposing the person to superfluous therapeutic by-products. In intensive care units, tests of the blood acidity are conducted all the time in an attempt to maintain the proper values and to immediately correct any deviation in order to prevent complications and death. The venous blood indicates the metabolic condition of the cells, and the arterial blood indicates the level of vitality that feeds them. Saliva indicates the condition of the digestive system, the balance of water in the body, the lymphatic system, and the functioning of the pancreas. Urine provides us with important information on the kidney function, the balance of water, and the quantity of the electrons (energy) excreted together with essential materials and waste.

The correct values of rH among people full of vitality in their twenties are:

	pH	rH	(R) Ohms
Blood	7.30–7.35	21.5–23.5	190–210
Saliva	6.50–6.75	21.5–23.5	180–220
Urine	6.50–6.80	22.5–24.5	30–45

This technique can allow us to examine every fluid from the animal and vegetable world. It is thus possible to assess the values of the various fluids, such as fruit and vegetable juices that are suitable for correcting deviations in the biochemical platform, returning the biological system to an optimal balance (homeostasis).

Neutralizing the Acidity in the Blood through Food

Each component in our food can produce an acidic or basic reaction in the kidneys. The total of all the components after a meal or at the end of the day will determine the balance of acidity and alkalinity. The more components in our food that cause an acid reaction, the greater the acidic burden in the body. If the food contains components that cause a basic reaction, they will cause a high basic burden on the kidneys.

Food is divided into four main groups according to the level of acidity:

- food with a strong acidic reaction, such as meat, fish, and soft and hard drinks
- food with a slight acidic reaction, such as nuts, legumes, and seeds
- food with a slight basic reaction, such as fruit and vegetables
- food with a strong basic reaction, such as green-leaved vegetables, broccoli, and spinach

Modern Western nutrition is based predominantly on an abundance of meat and fish, which leave acid waste in the body, such as nitrogen, phosphorous, chlorine, and sulfur.

A daily consumption of more than thirty grams of protein naturally creates acidity in the body, but the consumption in the Western world is far higher. This demands the involvement of the neutralizing system that starts with too much nitrogen in the cells and too much loss of potassium in the urine. Adding salt to food does not meet the need for neutralizing acidity because of the connection between chlorine and sodium.

The increase in the level of sodium in the cells causes the resting potential of the cell membrane to drop and can hasten the development of cancerous growths. Therefore, when the reserves of sodium in the blood are depleted, calcium enters the fray in order to neutralize the acidity. Hence a large quantity of meat on a fixed basis causes a decline in the calcium reserves; the body starts to use the calcium in the body, leading to osteoporosis and also hastening the development of cancerous growths.

The body is capable of utilizing a certain amount of amino acids for the protein needed by the cells. The excess amino acids decompose in the liver, are exploited for energy, and become fats, in which process they become ammonia excreted by the kidneys.

Examination of the pH in the urine can partially reflect the body's acid-basic balance. Acidic or basic urine beyond the normal values (pH = 6) indicates a lack of balance and poisoning of the organs and the various corporal systems. This does not testify necessarily to an illness, but if this is the ongoing situation, it is liable to be manifested as illness in the future.

Neutralizing the acidity in the Western diet without changing the energy consumption or the essential food elements can improve the health of the bone, improve the balance of protein and nitrogen, reduce the level of cholesterol in the blood, encourage anabolism, minimize catabolism, increase the production of the thyroid gland hormone, and prevent resistance to the growth hormone.[78] Thus, one has to act prior to the appearance of the illness by:

- adding basic minerals to the diet: such as cesium, rubidium, and potassium, which neutralize the acids and afford a supportive treatment for cancerous growths[79]
- adding potassium bicarbonate ($KHCO_3$) can replace sodium bicarbonate to neutralize the acidity, which is found to be effective in creating a negative nitrogen balance[80]
- consuming fruit and vegetable juices; fruit and vegetable juices are useful for raising the level of vitality and neutralizing acids in the blood, especially among people with a low level of vitality, such as when depressed or suffering from chronic fatigue syndrome or a drop in sexual functioning and cancerous growths. Since one cannot eat a quantity of vegetables that is equal to seven cups of juice daily, one can drink their juice. Measuring the acidity in the urine allows one to determine the acid or basic burden of the food on the kidneys and the level of acidity excreted in the urine. Thus, it is possible to choose suitable food that can correct unwanted deviations.[81]

  However, if one eats particularly large breakfasts, including carbohydrates and meat that generate a high acidic reaction, and basic foods cannot be added to the meal, a small amount of glutamine can be taken (thirty grams divided into five portions a day), which can neutralize the acidity somewhat.[82]

practicing transcendental meditation to lower acidity: Stress raises the tension in the muscles, increases the heart rate and metabolic rate and produces acid waste (like lactic acid and uric acid). In contrast, meditation enables good and deeper sleep, lowers the level of tension, and neutralizes acidity, thus improving health and preventing the development of degenerative illnesses or cancer. Studies show that transcendental meditation lowers the frequency of cancerous growths by 55 percent and the total cost to the health system by 53 percent.[83]

Earth Element

The earth element stabilizes, strengthens, and preserves. Its attributes are stability, slowness, sleepiness, dullness, lack of energy, weakness, drowsiness, heaviness, and obduracy that provides the body shape, a quiet appearance, lack of movement, and posture with invisible downward movements.

In the organism, it is concentrated in the brain, the liver, the spleen, excrement, the gall bladder, the bile duct, the kidneys, and the urinary tract and is distributed by blood through the body.

Excrement is the secretion of the undesirable element of earth and its excess.

When the earth element is in harmony with the other elements, it generates coherence, stability, masculinity, gratitude, understanding, tolerance, body strength and weight, durability, length of life, short-term memory, sleep, and lack of avarice.

- People with an excess of the earth element are heavy and slow in their movements and thoughts, and they often store poisons in the tissues. A surfeit results in accumulations and blockages, and therefore, the content of the digestive system becomes tough, moves slowly, and creates blockages, as occurs with stones in the large intestine, the gall bladder, the saliva glands, and the kidneys. It also promotes the creation of calcium deposits in the organs and atherosclerosis. An excess of the earth element is manifested in avarice and greed.

- Deficiency and disharmony in the earth element create instability, atrophy, lack of patience and understanding, weakness in the connecting tissues (loss of minerals), demineralization of the bones (osteoporosis), and cell atrophy.

Biomechanical Energy

Biomechanical energy is the energy needed to produce work. In their daily performance, our bodies function with the help of balanced and suitable operating systems, such as the skeleton and the muscles, the nervous system, the sensory system, and the heart-lung system. These systems are responsible for our posture and balance and our coordination and efficient exploitation of energy. Biomechanical energy is needed for the maintenance of these systems, providing us with the ability to make a physical effort and enabling us to perform various activities, from regular walking through running and participating in sports. The availability of biomechanical energy enables us to develop physical fitness.

Physical fitness is based on:

- cardiopulmonary endurance
- strength
- muscle endurance
- flexibility
- speed and rapidity

Cardiopulmonary endurance is defined as a person's ability to persist in submaximal efforts for a lengthy period of time. A farmer in the field, a teacher in school, or a surgeon in a hospital must have good cardiopulmonary endurance. Their ability enables the body to absorb larger quantities of oxygen that enter the lungs from the air and transport it using the blood through the arteries to all the cells, when the motivating and pushing force of the blood is the heart. Regular physical activity that maintains cardiopulmonary endurance causes an increase in the level of vitality in all the tissues and enables easy secretion of the waste materials, which are transported back to the lungs and other systems and expelled. Consequently, those with a high cardiopulmonary endurance rate have a significantly lower rate of heart and blood-vessel disease.

Strength is the ability to lift a very heavy weight one time, for example, moving a washing machine. This activity is tiring and demands a period of time before that strength can be used again. All sporting activity starts by using strength: when an athlete jumps, runs, or swims, he or she must apply force, measured as the degree of strength that must be applied in order to carry a given weight or the degree of strength needed to accelerate the body (provide it with speed or to alter it).

Muscle endurance is defined as the ability to repeat the same activity many times without tiring. For example, carrying heavy bags with both hands and walking a long distance, playing football for a whole hour, or walking for half an hour requires high muscle endurance. The combination of the strength and cardiopulmonary endurance will be manifested particularly in competitive sports, such as a bicycle race or a marathon.

Endurance is the combination of muscle strength and muscle endurance. The opposition in muscle endurance exercises is usually relatively low, and therefore, the push-up, pull-up, and sit-up exercises are considered strength-endurance exercises since opposition is high and the length of performance is relatively long.

Flexibility is the ability to relax a muscle that is not needed for a particular activity. This is an active process that demands energy. Thus, for example, flexibility in the heart muscle enables it to recover quickly from the contraction stage in order to be ready for the next contraction.

A lack of flexibility affects the heart's relaxation and consequently lowers its functional ability. Flexibility allows us to turn our heads while driving without our necks getting caught, to bend over to lift an object without back pain, or clench our fists and bend the knees without joint pain. The combination of energetic availability and flexibility allow us rapid movement.

The source of biomechanical energy in the muscles is the conversion of biochemical energy. The only energy that the muscle is capable of exploiting is that released when one of three groups of phosphates splits from energy-rich ATP and is converted to ADP. During physical activity, the ATP is recomposed due to the energy released from decomposing the energy-rich material—the creatine-phosphate (CP). If it were not for this material, the activity would have to be halted after six seconds because of the lack of ATP in the muscle. The energy that these two compounds are capable of providing can maintain intense activity for twenty seconds. This is the ATP/CP system.

The moment this system is recruited (and the concentration of material that feeds it begins to drop) two additional systems are drafted on two different tracks to provide energy and renew the supply of CP. The anaerobic system, which decomposes glucose into pyruvic acid that afterward becomes lactate or lactic acid, works faster. This process releases energy that is enough for twenty seconds to two minutes of activity, such as running four hundred meters, lifting weights several times, and push-ups. The increase in the concentration of lactic acid will suppress the ability to continue activity. At the same time, the aerobic track also starts functioning, in which the glucose serves as fuel but is assisted by oxygen in order to decompose it into carbon dioxide and water—waste materials that are easily expelled. Glycolysis can also use fats, decompose the pyruvic acid—and thus prevent its conversion to lactic acid—and even decompose into carbon dioxide and water. Thus, this track has no side effects and is not limited as long as biochemical energy is available.

Physical Activity and Lactic Acid

When oxygen levels are not sufficient, pyruvate is converted into lactate in our muscles. Usually a concentration of lactic acid of two moles per liter or less is a sign that the aerobic system easily meets the demands. When the concentration is between two and four moles per liter, the aerobic system is dominant but is assisted by the glycolysis system, and when higher than four moles per liter, it is a sign that the glycolysis system meets its main need and the concentration should be expected to rise as activity continues. Every person has a maximum ability in which there is a tremendous jump in the accumulation of lactic acid, which the body finds very hard to handle, and it is therefore quickly burned by the muscles to the point that it is simply impossible to continue at the same pace.

This maximum ability is connected to age and is measured by calculating the maximum heart rate and deducting the age from 220. Thus, for example, the maximum heart rate for a twenty-year-old male is 200; for a man age forty, it is 180. (it is recommend using the figure of 200 instead of 220 for women.)

A more significant increase in lactic acid occurs when we reach 65 percent of our maximum ability—rising from 2.2 moles per liter at 65 percent of the target pulse to 4 moles per liter at 80 percent. This threshold of 80 percent of the target pulse is termed the "anaerobic threshold."

Physical activity above the anaerobic threshold, or a very lengthy effort, causes overtiredness as a result of diminished pools of energy and the accumulation of waste (such as lactic acid) in the tissues.

If we wish to extend the activity time without altering the level of output (the rate at which certain work is performed), we will have to increase the amount of energy we use. In order to increase output, we have to increase the rate at which oxygen is transferred from the lungs to the active muscles or raise the anaerobic threshold. Another means is to generate change in the muscle cells that will enable more efficient exploitation of the oxygen flowing to them. This can be attained through extended moderate physical activity. However, short-burst training is confirmed to be healthy, as we will discuss later.

When we function at a capacity that enables the aerobic system to cover the ongoing consumption of energy, the concentration of lactic acid in the blood will be fixed. At the start of activity, it rises slightly but stabilizes when the acidic system reaches a level of activity that covers the ongoing needs. If the aerobic system's ability is greater than the ongoing consumption, the concentration will drop and the excess generated at the beginning of the activity will serve as fuel for its continuation. However, if the energetic needs are greater than what the aerobic system is capable of providing, the shortage will be filled by the glycolitic system and the concentration of lactic acid in the blood will rise.

Physical Fitness

The aspects of physical fitness develop, mature, and fade in stages. From the age of forty, the functional abilities (connected to the various corporal systems) decline.

Regular physical activity fills a key function in the quality of life and a person's health. It does not need to be measured in performance ability but in persistence and in the diversity of activities. Practicing the use of strength counters aging processes, manifested in weakness and atrophy of the muscles, but improves muscle tone and prevents a variety of orthopedic problems as well as osteoporosis. The more we exercise, the higher the VO_2 values (volume of oxygen that the body consumes every moment during physical exercise at sea level), which enables transporting a larger amount of oxygen to the cells and producing more energy needed for aerobic effort.

Practicing potency affords the human body vitality, the ability to perform daily tasks, and stable health. Research shows that this contributes directly to increasing self-confidence and to a feeling of self-capability. Furthermore, it improves the external appearance and the posture and thus physical, emotional, and social balance.

Regular physical activity among adults is very important for the persona and for society. Thus, for example, when the West German government discovered in the mid-seventies that about half the health budget was invested in hospital geriatric departments, professional committees were established whose role it was to locate means, tools, and ways of reducing costs. One of the clear conclusions was that "One has to get the people going"; thus plans were drawn up for physical activity and for public relations, and in less than a decade, the investment in those departments dropped by more than half (i.e., finding activities for the elderly lowered the rate of illness).

Moderate Physical Activity
and a Healthy Lifestyle

In recent years, considerable scientific proof has amassed showing that moderate physical activity, at least three times a week, has a long-term impact on reducing the risk of illnesses, such as heart and blood vessel disease, diabetes, and cancers.

A healthy lifestyle also includes a low-calorie, low-fat diet rich in vegetables and fruits, with limited consumption of natural fat and fried food. The consumption of sweet foods, such as sweets and chocolate, that are not useful for ongoing physical activity, should be restricted while food rich in carbohydrates that are digested and absorbed gradually and combined with the controlled use of olive oil, canola oil, and tahini (sesame sauce) can provide good energy for performing physical activity and maintaining health. Alcohol should also be avoided—or restricted to at the most a glass a day—and the consumption of coffee restricted; however, a coffee enema could be used to increase the vital energy of muscles. It is worth noticing that moderate physical activity reduces stress, while anaerobic activity increases the muscle mass and the energy-producing tissue and therefore the vitality, as will be discussed later in this book.

Tests to Assess Biomechanical Energy

Biomechanical energy can be assessed by evaluating muscular endurance, which is usually specific to each group of muscles; thus, no one test can assess the body's general endurance strength. Therefore, in order to obtain a picture of general endurance and physical strength, we recommend including tests from the upper and the lower limbs and the torso.[84]

The muscular strength test checks the static (isometric) force of the muscles through flexing and releasing the palm using a hand-grip dynamometer (whose grip is adapted to the size of the participant's palm). The decision whether to perform the test with the dominant hand or with each hand separately is usually taken in advance; thereafter, the average score is calculated (for many, there is a difference of 5 to 10 percent between the two hands). The test is considered cheap, mobile, and particularly reliable, although there is also a high correlation between the test and muscle mass.[85]

The strength of the grip tends to be higher among those with an earth build, who are usually taller and heavier.[86]

Factors that Determine the Elements' Quantities

The energy of the elements exists in the human being when he or she is in balance and depends on three main factors:

- the quantity of basic energy received from the parents
- the quantity of energy received from the external environment
- the quality of energy secreted by the various organs

The quantity of basic energy is that with which we are born and is determined by our parents' corporal, emotional, and the energetic condition at the moment of fecundation and by the energetic state during pregnancy. The parents' energetic condition is affected by several factors, including their health, their nutrition, and the emotional and energetic state of their place of residence. Thus, for example, if the father's energy at fecundation is of the air and earth type and the mother's energy is of the air and fire type, the child will be born with the fire, air, and earth attributes.

The energetic condition of the parents' elements at the moment of fecundation does not necessarily fit with their genetic condition. If, for example, the father has the elementary attributes of air and earth, but fecundation was during the summer heat (excess fire) and he ate spicy foods and drank hot drinks (excess fire), his body, at that time, had additional fire over and above the basic air and earth, and the embryo will receive the three elements from the father. This explains the difference between siblings from the same parents who have the same genetic onus. The energetic structure that was transmitted during fecundation defines which genetic traits will be manifested in the baby.

Therefore, if in the period of pregnancy, the organ responsible for secreting a particular element was defective and the parent had a surfeit of this element, this excess will affect the physical attributes and the embryonic development. For example, if the kidneys do not function, there will be excess water in the body, which will create physical, psychic, emotional, and functional imbalances in the mother and affect the embryo.

The parents' genetic factors, the nutrition, and the mother's activity during pregnancy, the internal condition of the womb, and the birth canal all affect newborns but are considered secondary factors compared to the basic energetic structure of the elements.

If we take into consideration the physical and mental attributes of each element, we will be able to identify diverse combinations. The human build shows us what a person's base attributes are. Indeed, if we take into consideration the four basic elements, we will be able to discern four types of build: the fire, the air, the water, and the earth builds. No one has a pure build of one basic attribute, but when we refer to a specific build, such as the earth build, we imply that the earth element is dominant relative to the other elements and is manifested at the person's physical and emotional planes.

Theoretically, we should be balanced and embrace all four elements in a harmonious manner. But in fact, there is no person in the universe who totally contains the four elements equally. The diverse concentrations lead to the infinite differences between people. An excess or shortage of one of the elements will affect the body build and the emotional and spiritual traits.

Every energetic imbalance is expressed in the specific attributes of the unbalanced element, whether at the corporal or the emotional plane. When the body is healthy, the person's adaptive ability is good and the digestive system active; metabolic excess does not remain in the body. In contrast, excess remains in the body when a person is sick, which disturbs his or her normal functioning.

The third factor that determines the level of each element in the body is the secretion of these elements by the organs intended for this. Each element has one or more organs that are responsible for secreting the excess element in order to maintain a proper balance. If this organ does not function properly, the quantity of the element in the body will be exaggerated and be manifested in a lack of balance in the system. The prayer "He Who created …" said by observant Jews after using the bathroom stresses this aspect: "Blessed art thou O Lord our God, king of the universe, who hast formed man in wisdom and created in him many orifices and vessels. It is revealed and known before the throne of thy glory that if one of these be opened or one of those be closed, it would be impossible to exist and o stand before thee. Blessed art thou, O Lord, who healest all flesh and doest wondrously."

Secretion and the Balance Mechanism

The body has four modes of secretion that maintain the balance between the four elements: perspiration and secreting digestive juices ensure the balance of fire; the air we exhale and secrete from the body through the gasses of the large intestine balances the quantity of air; urine facilitates the balance of water; and excrement maintains balance in the earth element.

The condition of the secretions can testify to the lack of energetic balance, and each element—and organ that is connected to it—needs four balanced elements.

Secreting the Air Element

The air that is exhaled is our body's way of preserving the balance of the element of air. It does not necessarily have an unpleasant smell, and excretion of feces should be minimal. A surfeit of this element leads to an excess of stomach gas and consequently to sensitivity to wind and cold that can result in catching a chill. An excess of the fire element dries out the respiratory tract. It is manifested in heavy breathing that is sometimes connected to mechanical obstacles because of a serious infection of the upper respiratory tract, such as the epiglottis (causing difficulties in exhaling air and stridor, a high-pitched sound resulting from turbulent air flow in the upper airway). An excess of the element of water leads to excess secretion from the lung mucous and bronchi (bronchitis) that can be manifested as a blockage in the respiratory tract, with a wet cough and difficulty in exhaling. An excess of the earth element leads to heaviness, breathing difficulties, and impermeability of the pharynx, as happens to obese people who sleep badly and are chronically tired.

Secreting the Fire Element

Perspiration is the means of secretion that is responsible for balancing fire in the body. It usually occurs when the climate is hot and after physical effort, tastes salty, and slightly moistens the skin in order to protect its flexibility and moisture. People with an excess of the fire element suffer from heat; those with reddish skin perspire easily, and their perspiration is hot and plentiful with a strong smell. A lack of the fire element is manifested in a lack of perspiration, and it is also connected to an excess of air so that the skin feels cool even when it is very hot.

An excess of the water element leads to excess cold sweat without a salty taste. A surfeit of the earth element will result in dry, tough, thick, and inflexible skin with little perspiration.

Secreting the Water Element

Urine is the method of excretion for maintaining the balance of the water element. Proper observation of the quantity, color, and smell of the urine helps diagnose the balance of the other elements. Normal urine is light yellow with a slightly acidic smell. An excess of water dilutes it so that it becomes clear like water, almost without smell, and plentiful. An excess of the fire element manifests in a yellow color, with a burning sensation when urinating despite the large quantity of urine and the absence of bacteria in the bacteriological test. This is different from a lack of the water element, which is manifested in sparse, dark urine that does not burn. An excess of the earth element can cause stones in the urinary tract.

Secreting the Earth Element

Excreting feces is the means of maintaining the balance of the earth element. Healthy feces should be semisolid, soft, not sticky, banana-shaped, floating, free of undigested food, and not too dark, without mucus or a strong smell. Observation of feces can help us to discern a lack of energetic balance or disturbance in the digestive process; an unpleasant smell and feces that sink in water testify to decay as a result of a lack of the fire element and surfeit of the water element (that leads to difficulties in digesting protein). Too dark a color testifies to the excess in the air element (exposing the feces to the air darkens them), and a yellowish color testifies to excess of the fire element. Feces full of mucus or fluid testify to the excess of the water element; hard feces testify to the excess of the earth element and lack of water.

Disturbance in the functioning of an organ that is responsible for excretion will lead to the accumulation in the body of the element that was to be excreted. Thus, for example, a disturbance in exuding perspiration can cause a high fever; a disturbance in exuding air will lead to overexpansion of the lungs (emphysema); a disturbance in excreting water through the kidneys can cause edema in the body; and a disturbance in excreting feces and constipation can cause an accumulation of poisons in the tissue and their hardening.

Personalized Medicine

Personalized medicine is a medical model that proposes the customization of health care using molecular analysis—with medical decisions, practices, and/or products being tailored to the individual patient. In this model, diagnostic testing is often employed for selecting appropriate and optimal therapies based on the context of a patient's genetic content. Science is trying to unravel the secrets of our genetic code, but only in a general one-size-fits-all model. Therefore, conventional medicine does not offer, or rarely offers, an integrative view of the body as a whole, linking body, mind, and soul.

The psychological aspect is not separate from the physical or the spiritual. The human code is the system that allows us to take consideration of the unique pattern of the magnetoelectric field of the animal soul. This is described as a constitutional human code. However, the code of the human soul determines the mental aspect, while the guiding spirit human code determines the intuition and creativity of the subject. The animal soul code is determined by the physical traits of the subject, while the code of the human soul is in the quantum realm and determined from the date of the birthday. The guiding spirit code is related to the person's name and the mother's name. In order to use this, I created software by which we can calculate the codes of the human soul and the guiding spirit in order to understand the nature of the person, the origin of moral and psychological suffering, and to guide him or her in the right path of intellectual fulfillment and spiritual evolution. In this book, I'll speak briefly about the way we obtain the human code; however, for further detail, see the *Human Code* book.

We have, until now, discussed the human biological constitution, but we have still not defined it exactly. The universal code enables us to refer to this from a unique perspective that allows dividing the biological constitution into sixty-four main types, in order to facilitate our intervention when necessary and to help people in a way suitable to their bodies, personalities, and souls.

The parameters scored for particular features include the following: facial structure, forehead shape, hair color, hair texture, eye color, eye shape, nose shape, nose profile, teeth, chin, skin texture, eyebrows, ears, mouth, and lips or the like. Scoring may be accomplished by comparing to a gold standard to determine the relative membership to a particular parameter type of the elemental group. Once all features have been scored and identified, it will allow understanding of the physiological function, the emotional aspects, and the impact of the outside environment and of food on the specific person.

Our bodies are a tool for our souls and have the ability to continue developing throughout life. We can thus define life as a transition period between the soul's last incarnation and the next. Our bodies and our psyches are influenced by many factors, from the moment of fertilization until our corporal death.

The human body comprises a combination of materials that we introduce to ourselves through food, air, and light, as well as through love and electromagnetic energy. Four types of energy can be identified that are identical to the four elements: earth, water, air, and fire, each of which has basic qualities that affect the body build, its movement, and its physiological functioning.

The essence of the four elements and the differences between them, their combinations, and the impact of the external factors determine each person's physical, emotional, and mental attributes.

Since each element has unique attributes, people can be characterized according to the degree to which each element is manifested therein to describe him or her physically and emotionally and even to predict his or her behavior and the way in which he or she will cope with emotional crises. Each person has a code that is compatible with one of the sixty-four universal codes.

These attributes appear at the first stages of the embryonic development and determine the rate and type and the weight and morphology of body development. Indeed, one can identify the human type almost immediately after birth. When we identify the category to which the child belongs, we can draw conclusions regarding his or her traits and behavior, accept him or her as he or she is and encourage him or her in the direction suitable to him or her. We can thus exploit his or her personal potential on the one hand and provide him or her with the elements that compensate for those missing on the other hand. Indeed, the food and living environment can be altered to attain balance, and environmental pollution, electromagnetic radiation, and so on can be reduced. Of course, our ability to influence is limited.

These basic attributes are dynamic and can be altered according to the person's developmental stage, to the climate in which he or she lives, the food he or she eats, and his or her emotional condition. Our recognition of our physical and emotional build allow us to choose our lifestyle and adapt it to the personal makeup of each of us and thus to maintain our health.

Anyway, the constitutional human code is a method for diagnosing and identifying the state of well-being and harmony of an individual based on external markers, such as that of body and/or facial characteristics. The diagnosis is accomplished by determining a unique human code that is abstracted from the body and facial characteristics of an individual in order to look at the whole person, including an analysis of physical, emotional, social, spiritual, nutritional, and environmental and lifestyle values.

Each human being is carrying extraordinary potential of expression to become open and accomplished beings. The human code is a code that is able to characterize an individual. We can directly examine and analyze the facial morphology and stratify the total population into different subsets, each with common but unique characteristics. It makes it possible to go very far in the study of the process of operation psychic.

How Does One Determine a Person's Physique and Psychological Type?

The basic principle determining the identification of a person's physique is the universal energetic code according to which each person is unique since he or she is the result of the endless combination of physique, biological build, animal soul, and guiding spirit. The chance of finding two people who have had the same experiences not only in this life but also in previous lives, received the same genetic components from their parents, and were accompanied by an identical guiding spirit is zero. At the same time, we often encounter a person who reminds us of another person. This similarity stems from the resemblance in biological components that can cause them to behave in similar manner and even to develop similar illnesses.

Conventional medicine claims a person's external appearance and physique are irrelevant, and therefore the latter is not important and has no connection to illnesses. However, as we have seen previously, the physique is a direct manifestation of energy and the human soul that affect the type of behavior and the attraction of the outside world. There is therefore a direct connection between the spiritual and emotional components and the physical appearance.

Observations and diagnoses of an individual are based on external body markers that determine individual characteristics, personality traits, health state, mental health, personal psychology, and vulnerabilities, as well as talents, strengths, gifts, and abilities. It provides not only a framework for understanding human life itself but very specific knowledge about each individual. This is about technique and human sciences that allow interpreting and analyzing a character, based on a body's form and face features. When the analysis is well developed, it reveals the person's concealed potential, and as such, it helps in developing it.

The human code can be specific to your personal genetic formula. The information in the human code is presented by six members composed of two or more parameter groups, which are marked with a plus or a minus sign. The upper two members represent the polarity associated with an individual, while the lower four members represent the elemental portion of the code comprising physiological energies: biochemical, bioelectric, biomechanical, and biomechanical energy. The sign used to represent elemental features indicates the presence or absence of an elemental feature associated with a face. For example, an addition sign (+) indicates the presence of an element while a minus sign (−) indicates the absence of an element. The upper member determines the dominant polarity of a subject. The code's polarity portion is similarly represented, preferably indicating the type of polarity rather than presence or absence. The human code represents your mind, your emotions, your heart, and your intuition, and the rhythms and patterns that govern your movement through life.

The combination of the attributes that are connected by polarity to the attribute four elements presents us with sixty-four types, similar to the universal energetic code. This combination provides a sources of many and diverse traits, and enables us to diagnose a person better and note the possibilities for treatment in order to attain renewed health and balance. The many possibilities, relationships, and attributes explain the great variety in type.

The physical build and facial shape afford a base tool through which we can distinguish nature and determine code. Each of the sixty-four types has a suitable facial structure that evinces certain energies, abilities, and possible health problems.

Each type is based on filters that determine a person's *temperament*, which causes him or her to behave in a particular way and presents him or her with crises of a particular type, through which he or she learns to progress in life and to develop spiritually. Recognizing the type enables the doctor and the therapist to identify the natural forces embedded in the patient and his or her real potential, and to guide him or her to exploit this natural potential and to abandon efforts to deviate from his or her natural tendencies.

This can be compared to swimming with the stream in a river, which enables considerable progress with minimal energetic investment instead of swimming against the stream and fighting it. When we are familiar with our physique, we know how to behave in a way that is compatible with it, causing us to feel full of life and vitality despite life's difficulties and the obstacles.

This is an important tool for doctors, psychologists, and therapists. It enables us to understand the patient's nature, predict his or her behavior and discern his or her weak emotional and physical points, and to adapt the therapeutic approach to the individual.

Learning the build and type affords a basis that offers the doctor meaningful therapeutic possibilities and enables individual treatment for every patient, differentiating between functional disturbances and illnesses stemming from an inner source and external disturbances that reveal or exacerbate the problem. These will allow the patient to understand him- or herself and to apply his or her ambitions in a way that is compatible with his or her biological and spiritual nature (i.e., to flow in the direction and way that the laws of nature support him or her and his or her deeds, or in religious terms, to do God's will). Unfortunately, only a few lucky people in our midst have identified the correct way that flows in the natural direction of their possible realms. I frequently meet people who are involved in professions and circumstances that are not compatible with their build or nature, some of them for convenience and others for financial reasons. Some of them actually earn much money but are dissatisfied and suffer emotional distress. The suffering, which includes physical illness, is intended to guide people and to indicate the problematic areas in which they have deviated from the path suitable to their objective. In my opinion, the doctor should be aware of this and be capable of decoding these signs in order to help the patient to find his or her path. Knowing our type will teach us to accept what we are, and thus, we will be able to develop the natural potential embedded within us without suffering from what does not pertain to us.

The human code offers an interpretation of each frame, feature, type, and zone compared to the face as a whole and to other features and zones as well. It gives us a strategy for living life authentically. It can tell us why we are with the people we are with. It can tell us what we have always been seeking and where we have been conditioned to be other than ourselves. It's not about changing who we are, but recognizing who we have always been. The human code can bring about such a transformation. It empowers us with very specific information about our genetic makeup so that we can regain trust in ourselves to know how and when to act, what decisions will work best for us, and what is most important in our life. As in any human science, the human code is based on a technique, intuition, humanity, and psychological maturity of the person who is practicing it.

The human code excels as tool for diagnosis and is highly advised for psychology and medicine professionals. Support for better communication, it can help any person in relation to working with the public. This science helps in human relations, in children's education, in any professional life (productive and cooperative relations), in human resources (training and direction to take), as well as sentimental life, as it teaches one to see oneself and see the other, understand oneself and understand the other, discover oneself and discover the other in his or her positive inclinations and focus, without referring to negative inclinations, which may spoil one's life. Invaluable support of self-knowledge, it is a fundamental personal progress instrument.

New Definitions of the Basic Concepts in Medicine

Integrative medicine is described as more than just the sum of conventional medicine plus CAM.[87]

Maizes et al. define *integrative medicine* as "healing-oriented medicine that reemphasizes the relationship between patient and physician, and integrates the best of complementary and alternative medicine with the best of conventional medicine."[88]

This book defines the term somewhat similarly, placing emphasis on use of evidence. However, in biomedical model the evidence is based on the conventional endpoint, which is based on objective parameters that can be measured, such as body temperature, pulse rate, breathing rate, blood pressure, biochemical tests of the blood, and other laboratory tests. Therefore, the purpose of the treatment is to attain normal values, without trying to assess the environmental conditions and emotional and mental stress caused by family conflicts, work difficulties, economic crises, and so on. Therefore, there is no place for psychological, social, and spiritual wellbeing. According to this model, the disease within the body is caused externally; the person who is ill is assumed to be the passive victim of the disorder and not responsible for his or her illness. Therefore, the treatments are an external intervention that will cure the disease, and the patient is a passive recipient of treatment with only a minor role to play, if any.

Therefore, the integration with complementary and alternative medicine fails in the definitions and model of conventional medicine. It is time to change from the root of the model by changing the definition and constructing a model that takes seriously the three components of the person: body, psyche, and soul.

The basic concepts that should be changed and newly defined are homeostasis, well-being, the state of health, malaise, and disease.

Homeostasis

A living organism is thermodynamically an open system, which is operating out of and often far from, thermodynamic equilibrium in an environment with which it exchanges energy and matter conferring a dynamic quality to the living organism. The dynamic equilibrium that the living system needs in order to maintain the state of health and this balance is called homeostasis.

We can therefore, define homeostasis as **a state of dynamic equilibrium by which the system functions in full order with minimal energy expense**. The homeostasis depends on three main factors:

- the vitality of the physical body
- the free flow of energy in the system in four life phases.
- the resonance between the mental and emotional energy and the subject nature determined by the constitutional (animal soul) human code and human soul—the human code.

Therefore, it is important to determine the human code before starting the diagnosis and therapy. This will allow the therapist to understand what constitutes the individual's the personal well-being and create a personalized diagnosis and program of therapy.

Well-Being

Well-being is a step beyond homeostasis. In fact, homeostasis deals mainly with the state of function of the system, while well-being includes function and feeling.

Homeostasis depends on vitality and resonance with the biological constitution (human code), which means that the person is functioning in accordance with his or her biological and spiritual nature. Subjective well-being means experiencing good feelings due to three main factors:

- a sense of individual vitality
- realization of personal aspiration by doing meaningful, engaging activities, which make the person feel competent to satisfy needs and to be autonomous
- a stock of inner resources to help the person cope with difficulties and obstacles and be resilient to changes beyond his or her immediate control and being able to change or cope with the environment.

These three elements are found in the definition of health and health promotion by WHO:

> Health promotion is the process of enabling people to increase control over, and to improve, their health ...
> To reach a state of complete physical, mental and social well-being, an individual or group must be able

to identify and to realize aspirations, to satisfy needs, and to change or cope with the environment. (Ottawa Charter for Health Promotion, 1986)

Therefore, we can define well-being as follows: **A state of mind by which person feels able to fulfill his or her projects in life with sense of love, happiness, and freedom.** In this state, the biologic system is in homeostatic balance and functions well.

What Is Health?

The WHO defined health as a state of complete physical, mental, and social well-being; the well-being depends on a sense of free flow that allows the person to realize material aspiration and spiritual fulfillment.

Therefore, the new definition of health should take in the three components of the human being: body, soul, and psyche. We can define the state of health as follows: **a state of resonance between the psyche-spiritual energy (the soul) and the physical body by which the defense system (vitality) is able to cope with the external and internal stimuli efficiently to maintain homeostasis.**

The resonance manifests as a state of balance between the sympathetic and parasympathetic systems. The imbalance between the sympathetic and the parasympathetic is caused as a response to noxious physical and emotional stimuli. They provoke physical, mental, or emotional strain or tension, which in turn provokes a state of dissonance between the psychological intention and the basic nature. Not every stress causes a dissonance; only what is known as distress is negative and creates a state of dissonance that if not resolved could convert to disease.

The threshold that separates stress from distress is different from one person to other, and it depends on the state of vitality, which determines the defense system's resilience to cope with the external or internal stimulus. Chronic stress consumes energy, weakens the defense system, and leads to depletion of the vital force.

Therefore, to evaluate the state of health, we need to measure the state of tension by measuring the balance between the sympathetic and parasympathetic systems and by measuring the vital energy reserves.

The state of stress can be evaluated by measuring the balance between the sympathetic and parasympathetic system, while the vitality can be evaluated using the bioelectrical impedance analysis, especially measuring the *phase angle*, which was confirmed in its value for diagnosis and prognosis in a variety of different situations or by measuring the oxidative stress. One of the methods to measure the oxidative stress of the entire body is measuring the rH (relative hydrogen) of the blood.

Malaise

If there is dissonance between the soul and body, it will start to manifest as malaise.

Malaise is generally defined as a slight or general feeling of not being healthy or happy. However, we can be more specific, taking into consideration the three parts of the human being and define malaise as follows: **malaise is a state of dissonance between the psychospiritual state and body caused by an external or internal stimulus, with such an intensity that the defense system, although it is able to cope with it, has not yet reached the balance of homeostasis.**

If the state of malaise goes on and we do not act to identify and remove the cause, it may turn into disease. Before manifestation of disease, we have enough signs and time to intervene to correct the dissonance by resolving the emotional crisis and completing the learning process.

When we speak about malaise, we mean signs and symptoms that are not related directly to physical or mental illness. Mostly, we speak about symptoms without physical or mental disease.

The symptoms of malaise can include abdominal pain or cramping, enlarged lymph nodes without evidence of infection or tumor, fever, and chills, flu-like symptoms (fatigue, fever, sore throat, headache, cough, aches, and pains), joint pains, missed or irregular menstrual periods, muscle aches, severe fatigue, unexplained weight loss.

Malaise can occur along with anxiety; changes in mood, personality, or behavior; depression; difficulty with memory, thinking, talking, comprehension, writing, or reading; fatigue, irritability and mood changes, lack of energy, and lethargy.

Many of the symptoms of malaise are related to a lack of vitality, and the symptoms disappear completely by charging the body with vital energy as we will see.

It is very important to listen to the signs of malaise in order to resolve the dissonance created by psychological conflict and distress and to prevent disease development.

The Disease

Generally, the accepted definition of *disease* is a condition of the subject or of one of its parts that impairs or modifies normal vital functions and is typically manifested by distinguishing signs and symptoms. It is a response to environmental factors (such as malnutrition, industrial hazards, or climate), to specific infective agents (such as worms, bacteria, or viruses), to inherent defects of the organism (such as genetic anomalies), or to combinations of these factors.

This definition emphasizes the response of the system to external environmental factors; there is no mention of the state of mind or the well-being of the subject.

Therefore, the new definition of disease is: **a state of dissonance between the psychospiritual state and the physical body caused by external or internal stimuli with such intensity that exceeds the capacity of the defense system to restore the state of homeostasis.**

These definitions make it clear that there are two major factors that can put at risk the basic state of equilibrium. We consider as external stimuli the environmental factors that include all risk factors, which are in part already largely taken into account by conventional medicine, such as for example food quality, pathogenic factors like germs, carcinogenic factors, electromagnetic energy, radiation, sunlight, water quality, and so on. The endogenous factors, on the other hand, are not taken into great consideration or are even completely neglected in conventional medicine, except in genetic diseases. Internal stimuli belong to the psyche, as do psychological conflicts, endogenous psychological *stress*, and oxidative *stress*.

It appears clear, therefore, that in order to get to the disease, there must a combination of two main factors: a state of *dissonance* and a *failure of the defense system*.

By the term *defense system*, we do not mean only the immune system (which is part of the defensive complex) but also the basic vitality of the cells. The defense system is inversely correlated with oxidative *stress* and free radicals. The higher the oxidative *stress*, the lower the availability of vital energy in the cells and therefore the higher the risk of getting sick.

The Four Stages of Life and
the Four Stages of Stress

The state of dissonance is mainly caused by unresolved psychological conflicts that create a state of internal *distress* with different degrees threat. The psychological conflict causes an energy blockage in one of the four phases of life. From the nature of the disease, we can diagnose in which phase the block is and determine what kind of intervention should be done.

The advantage of this definition is that it indicates the cause of disease and not the response to different factors.

Our intervention is not intended to treat the symptoms and not even cure diseases, but instead to free the person from his or her conflicting limitations and energy blockages in order to complete the learning process and regain his or her psycho-physical-spiritual harmony, resume his or her journey, realize his or her fate, and feel happy despite the obstacles in life.

Therefore, we must understand what determines the vitality and the dissonance and resonance.

In my book, *The Seven Principles and the Seventh Sense*, I discussed the relation between the four stages of stress, the four life phases, and the four levels of fear. Stress is an event that has four stages, compatible with the four stages of life.

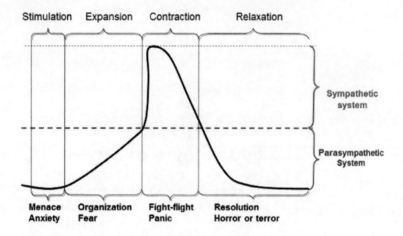

We can see in this diagram the relationship between the psychological conflict and the energy blockage.

It starts in an event occurring in the environment that creates a threat to the system (stimulus).

- Thereafter comes consideration of an event that involves organizing the defensive strengths (expansion).
- This is followed by action leading to an emotional/psychological and physical reaction, which is the stage of flight or fight (contraction).
- This concludes with the problem-solving stage (relaxation).

In order to illustrate the reaction to tension, let us take as an example the existential-territorial threat of an encounter between a deer and a lion.

Threat: The first moment of emotional tension raises emotional and nervous stimulation of the system. The approach of the lion to the deer's territory causes the latter concern and emotional-existential tension that makes it sensitive and aware of every outside change that is liable to be dangerous to its energetic, emotional, and physical system.

Physiological reaction: At this stage, the process of stimulating the autonomous nervous system mainly stimulates the adrenal gland and results in the secretion of adrenalin, noradrenalin, and cortisol.

- Physical reaction: The heart rate and blood pressure rise; there is increased flow of blood to the essential organs, such as the muscles and the brain.
- Psychological reactions: These include concern, increased awareness, disquiet, and disturbed sleep.

Organization: At this stage and after activating the autonomous nervous system, a general process of recruiting energies begins in order to convey the energy to the essential organs and systems in order to cope with the threat.

- Physiological reactions: A reaction in the brain causes the adrenal gland to secrete adrenalin, noradrenalin and cortisol, which recruit the body to immediate physical activity. Increasing the production of sugar and releasing sugar from the reserves to the blood flow provides energy to essential organs.
- Physical reactions: The blood vessels in essential organs, such as the heart, brain, muscles, and lungs expand. The breathing rate increases, and the bronchia dilate, bringing more oxygen to the brain and muscles. Stimulating the stress hormones secreted by the adrenal gland and the autonomous nervous system contracts the digestive and sexual systems; causes the blood vessels in the heart, the brain, the muscles, and the lungs to expand; the bronchia dilate; and the blood vessels of the skin contract.
- emotional reactions: At the organization stage and following activating the autonomous nervous system, the deer is fearful. It expands its chest in order to prepare for the next stage, which needs much energy, and also in order to scare the enemy by pretending it is bigger than it actually is.

Flight or fight: At this stage, the sympathetic system causes a rapid rise in the availability of energy to the body's essential organs.

- Physiological reactions: Contraction of the blood vessels in the digestive organs reduces the secretion of enzymes in the digestive system, the sex organs, and the skin; the blood's coagulation ability is accelerated; the production of energy and the retention of sodium in order to maintain the blood pressure are increased. Fear sometimes not only causes the contraction of the digestive and sex systems but also the loss of control of the sphincter, and urine and feces escape, facilitating the animal's escape and reducing its vulnerability. The corticosteroids with an anti-infectious affect increase; the adrenalin converts fatty acids and glycogen to sugar, and therefore, the level of blood sugar rises. The level of fats in the blood, including cholesterol and triglycerides, inflates; the parathyroid removes more calcium from the bones and transfers it to the brain and muscles; there is considerable destruction of protein in the lymph glands and the thymus and a drop in the functioning of the immune system.
- Physical reactions: Muscular contraction increases, the heart rate peaks, blood pressure is high, pupils dilate, and perspiration increases to lower the body temperature.
- Psychological reactions: There is fear and anxiety during which the deer's strength increases beyond its normal ability, in order to cope the most effectively with the threatening factor or to flee the danger.

The fourth stage can manifest itself in three ways, depending on the speed and intensity of the level of threat. All of them entail diverse degrees of relaxation, ranging from enjoyable relaxation through deep relaxation of exhaustion to the point of the absolute relaxation of shock and paralysis.

Solution (resolution): At this stage, after the emotional expression and threat have vanished, the body returns to the relaxed state, embarking on a process of correcting the damage and refilling the reserves of energy that emptied (especially at the third stage of flight or fight). The immune system starts functioning in order to correct possible damage due to the overcontraction of the tissues or due to direct harm by the threatening factor.

Psychological Conflict and Physical Disease

The peculiarity of this method is the relationship between the psychological conflict and malaise and physical disease. More than twenty-six years of experience have confirmed the great precision that allows us to understand better the personal predisposition for certain diseases and the biological terrain predisposition for external environmental factors, such as germs, radiation, and malnutrition.

The whole concept of disease or illness is often related to psychological crises that cause chronic stress and psychological and physical tension.

There are definite rules that allow us to make precise diagnoses and proper psychological and energy interventions to prevent disease development or to heal the existing disease.

As you saw earlier and from the new definition of disease, we don't wait for the manifestation of symptoms in order to treat them. We can make a very early diagnosis in the energy blockage stage to elaborate with the patient the psychological crises that was diagnosed, using the seventh sense that everybody can learn and develop in order to complete the learning process and achieve the state of well-being.

Emotions that have been repressed or unhealthily expressed are responsible for creating the biological terrain for disease development.

When a person holds in anger, fear, jealousy, etc., that emotional energy will be blocked according to very specific and fixed rules:

- The kind of psychological conflict determines which chakra will be involved. For example, if the emotional crisis is at home with a family member, it would be located in the chest; if it is related to work, it will be in the neck; if it is a social aspect, it will be in the abdomen, etc., causing a block in one of the energy centers or chakras.

- The level of fear during and after the emotional crisis determines in which of the four phases is the stress block—for example, anxiety related to work leads to hyperthyroidism, while fear leads to a goiter, panic from being dismissed will appear as nodules in the thyroid, overexpression or exhaustion at work could lead to hypothyroidism, and if the vitality of the thyroid is very low, it can lead to a malignant tumor of the thyroid.

- The person with whom we have the problem, male or female, determines which side, right or left, of the body that will be involved. For example, a conflict of separation from a beloved will block the energy in the heart; if the person involved is male, the right coronary artery will react to this kind of conflict, and if she is female, the left coronary artery will be involved.

- The modality of coping with the conflict will determine which meridian and related organ will be involved. For example, an unexpected dismissal from work that could not be digested will block the stomach's energy and block the stomach meridian. Fear of criticism from one's wife creates tension in the left side of the colon, and tension appears along the left colon meridian.

- The perception modality and trauma interpretation will determine which germ layer derivative tissue in the specific organ will be involved in the disease. Existential crises that are related to survival affect the tissues derived from the endoderm. A car accident that provoked deep trauma and fear of physical damage will involve the pancreas, which is derived from endoderm. Lack of sustenance and support will cause a reaction

258

in tissue derived from the mesoderm. Conflicts of separation and detachment will involve tissues derived from the ectoderm.

Knowing the organ and the histological tissue gives us the exact psychological event that caused the disease.

The modality of expression is divided into two main groups, each one with two phases. This division is important for the therapy plan.

The first group is related to emotional repression that causes a block in the first two phases of four phases of life. The emotional energy is held in the organ or the specific tissue related to the conflict. In this case, our therapy should be oriented to drain out the excess energy.

The second group is related to emotional overexpression, such as seen in rage-aholics. In this case, there is excessive loss of energy derived from the specific tissue related to the conflict and our therapy plane will be oriented to restore the energy loss.

Signs of Unbalanced Health: Excess Tension and Lack of Energy

> There is no healing for a sick person who believes he is healthy.
>
> —Frederick Amiel

Nervousness, restlessness, oversensitivity, paleness, despondency, and general discomfort are likely to stem from excess tension or lack of energy. It is important to differentiate between the two states as previously mentioned since the therapeutic approach to them is totally different.

The following is an example of loss of energy. A forty-year-old woman lost her husband in a road accident and became depressed. She did not cease crying, started to gain weight, lost interest in life, and started to suffer from general weakness, dizziness, and anemia. Her menstruation became irregular to the point of total cessation.

The following is another example of excess of tension. A forty-year-old man who was dismissed from his work closed himself into his house and ceased expressing his feelings. He became a heavy smoker and was nervous and impatient. He began to suffer from pain in his neck and shoulders, indigestion, and stomach pain (a stomach ulcer was discovered in a gastroscopy). He developed hyperlipidemia, and his blood pressure rose.

Two people of the same age both experienced a severe emotional trauma causing a lack of energy and a drop in the level of vitality (in the woman) or excess tension and stomach and shoulder cramps (in the man). Whence stem the differences in the symptoms?

As we have seen previously, every person is charged with energy that affords life and vitality to his or her tissues. This energy changes from day to day, its quantity and quality affected by internal and external environmental factors.

The internal factors depend on the mood and emotional crises that cause the energetic blockage, itself raising the level of emotional tension, and subsequently also increased tension in the tissues and diverse organs. This is manifested as contractions, pain, stomach ulcers, and problems in the small intestine (Crohn's disease) or the large intestine (ulcerative colitis) and even in the brain (multiple sclerosis(. The intensity of the contractions affects the mood and makes the person nervous, impatient, and unloving. This emotional state again affects the body and worsens the primary phenomena, generating a vicious cycle that only exacerbates the problem and makes the illness chronic.

In the course of time, the energetic blockages will cause a drop in the level of vitality—first in the specific organs and gradually in the general level of vitality to the point of the significant draining of the "battery." Subsequently, physical signs begin to appear in the tissue as well as a low mood, culminating in depression, disinterest, or the inability to function in order to alter the situation. Such deterioration necessitates intervention and outside help.

The external factors can worsen or alleviate the situation. For example, a person depressed after the loss of someone dear who eats food deprived of vitality (empty calories) will aggravate the depression. In contrast, the energetic condition of a person who is depressed but drinks fruit and vegetable juice, sleeps enough hours (usually more than is customary), and does not waste sexual energy will improve. Consequently, the period of depression will be brief and he or she will regain regular functioning.

Stress management

The treatment strategy will be discussed separately in the book on energy and emotion washout; however, some basic recommendations to reduce excess tension in general are reported here. The following will be beneficial:

- regular physical activity that will open the bronchial passages and increase perspiration
- a hot shower or a swim
- sexual activity with frequent orgasms (without ejaculation)
- emotional expression—enabling children in particular to express their anger and cry without limitation
- relaxation exercises, such as meditation, biofeedback, and yoga
- energetic and emotion washout (see *Energy and Emotion Washout*, www.naderbutto.com)

Level of Vitality

Considering that every function in our body and psyche needs energy to function, the more energy we have, the bigger our vital force and vitality will be. Our bodies are charged with life energy that is affected by many internal and external factors, each of which can charge or drain the battery.

We sometimes wake up in the morning without any desire to get out of bed or go to work, in a bad mood, with no strength, a low level of concentration, our memory not at its peak, and sexual desire and performance having known better days.

Sometimes, it is the exact opposite. We wake up livelier than ever and feel full of energy, as if we could conquer the world. The body functions energetically, the soul is uplifted, and we are full of love, patience, and understanding of others. In brief, we are full of energy.

Of which energy are we talking? How can we maintain a high level of energy all the time, be charged, and avoid energetic loss?

The situations described above cannot be measured or assessed according to biomedical model since both can reside together in every healthy person. In fact, every form of life is charged with a type of primal energy, similar to the magnetic energy that provides life and vitality. Indeed, far Eastern cultures, such as those in China, Japan, and India, consider life energies to be the basis for the existence of the world.

One of the important attributes of life energy is negative entropy (preventing the inner tendency of material to undergo a process of inner disorder and disintegration). In other words, life energy prevents the disintegration and disorder of the material. The higher the level of energy in the body and the better the materials are organized, the more likely illnesses are prevented and people live longer. However, it is not enough for the body to be charged with energy; this energy must also be dynamic, in constant motion, causing rhythmic expansion and contraction of the body's organs. Therefore, we need to design our lifestyles in accordance with all of our core values, balancing our energy expenditure and our energy income. So we need to know the origin of this energy and how we can maintain our battery's charge.

The Source of Vital Energy

The encounter between a man and a woman is polar, activating the flow of sexual energy and peaking in orgasmic relief. Such an encounter leads to a high concentration of energy around the pelvic area in order to cause fertilization of the egg by the sperm, its division in the womb, and its development into a healthy new being. Fertilization is a polar energetic process affording the energetic basis for embryonic development. The higher the couple's level of vitality, the greater the woman's chance of becoming pregnant and the healthier the embryo developing.

The level of embryonic vitality during pregnancy depends directly on the mother's level of vitality. Much love between the partners, emotional calm, correct nutrition, and good sleep are basic conditions for the woman's level of vitality to be high. During that period and the period immediately following the birth, the infant is fed by the mother's female energy, which charges the baby's female pole. The father's love and attention will enrich the male pole, and at the age of seven, both the child's poles—the male and the female—peak and generate the start of his or her sexual development.

At the age of twelve, the female pole peaks in girls and that of the male when he is fourteen years of age. This situation arouses sexual tension between boys and girls at these ages.

The strong flow between the main poles, one of which is located in the chest and the other in the pelvis (in males the polarity is counter to that of females) finds the poles remaining open and prepared for an additional charge. This occurs until the age of twenty-one approximately, when the long bones cease growing, the poles close, and the level of vitality declines until it is below a certain level—close to the end of life. From twenty-one to twenty-eight, the amount of energy is in steady state or plateau. After the age of twenty-eight, the energy starts to decrease and the aging process starts.

The external energy is absorbed in our bodies (through the centers of energy) through food (the animal and plant world), water, air (breathing), and the sun (light).

Food as a Source of vital Energy

The return to nature and to a healthy lifestyle, apparent in recent years, is in fact an overreaction to the industrialization that has taken over our world.

This industrialization is manifested in the expanded use of pesticides, in synthetic fertilizers, in giving medication to animals that we eat, and in genetic engineering. All these affect the quality of the environment, the soil, the water, the air, and even the food, which has lost its aroma, taste, and natural size. The path is therefore short from this to health problems that stem from eating animal products saturated with chemical materials and hormones.

Most of the synthetic fertilizers and pesticides used in agriculture are not materials that the body was exposed to for millions of years of human development, and therefore, the body finds them difficult to digest or secrete.

The cell needs suitable electromagnetic energy, with an identical frequency, to cope with and assimilate new material that enters it. However, the vital energy is dissipated while the food is being processed, and accordingly, these materials accumulate in the tissue and cause slow poisoning that affects its proper physiological functioning. Thus did the need for alternative agriculture and organic agriculture develop.

Organic agriculture is based on several principles:

- It does not use materials that are not of natural or plant origin. Animals or plants grow in their natural environment, without synthetic materials, such as hormones, pesticides, or chemical fertilizers, and the final product does not contain preservatives.
- Organic agriculture plots undergo a two- or three-year period of cleansing to remove the remains of conventional agriculture.
- The soil is fertilized with organic fertilizer from animal feces with the addition of natural mineral resources. Organic agriculture has developed methods of growing mixed crops (rows of different plants in the same field) to prevent the accumulation of insects that prefer a certain type of vegetable, thus greatly reducing the need for pesticides. Another method is altering the location of the planted vegetables from one season to another.

Despite the above, it has not yet been scientifically proven that organically grown products are healthier than conventional agricultural produce. The British Food Authority, directed by Professor John Krebs, adopts scientific criteria and, together with experts from the academic world, determines food standards for each stage of production and marketing. Krebs is not enthusiastic, to say the least, about organic products. This world-famous scientist said in September 2000 that "organic agriculture and its products are built on image, for which the consumer pays (as the prices of organic products are higher than for nonorganic products). Advantages have not yet been found in organic food compared to conventional food regarding the nutritional content of the materials or the level of chemical and other remains, despite the organic food produced in England being of a very high standard."

Another study conducted recently by the Swedish National Food Administration did not find any nutritional advantage to organic food.

Prof. Krebs also mentioned the British *WHICH* magazine of May 2003 that concludes, "There is no agreement regarding the reports about the health advantages of organic food." At the same time, he observed that scientific proof is a dynamic subject and reminded readers of the need to keep an open mind to every development or new finding.

It is important to note that the studies cited did not explore the aspects of the quality of the environment and the relationship to the earth and nature, which are an important component in the organic method and cannot be measured objectively.

But the main problem in the study conducted by the laboratory for the BBC and in other tests conducted is that they do not take into consideration a most important facet—the level of vitality of the food. Food that undergoes industrial processing admittedly includes the biochemical components (protein, carbohydrates, vitamins, etc.) but does not include life energy measurement. This could be measured using the Codix^R instrument that measures the rH and pH of the food and evaluates not only its antioxidant capacity but also its compatibility to each person. This is the point to note that processed food with organic components loses its vitality, exactly like food whose components are not organic. It is therefore worth thinking twice before buying processed organic food (at high cost) without knowing its vitality.

The amount of energy of each person depends on the balance between three factors: the amount of basic energy received from the parents; the energy received from outside sources; and the energy the body loses.

The amount of vital energy changes during life. Lucky people who received much love from their parents and the immediate surroundings will be full of this energy and accordingly will preserve it for many years, enjoy good health, and be resilient even if they do not follow a healthy lifestyle.

Removing the Waste from the Body and Conserving Good Energy

> Every organ draws the food it needs after it has been digested, and the waste excreted; for if the waste remains in us, it will become mouldy and lead to illness, God forbid.
>
> —Rambam

The natural purpose of the large intestine is to remove the excretions and poisonous materials originating in food, although modern life dictates to us a different rate to that planned for us by nature. Our eating culture includes exaggerated consumption of carbohydrates, meat, and other proteins from animal products; drinking water or soft drinks during meals, which dilutes the stomach acids and disturbs digestion; and combining proteins and carbohydrates in the same meal, disrupting the digestion of carbohydrates and of proteins.

The carbohydrates start to be digested by the saliva the moment they enter the mouth and thereafter in the duodenum and the small intestine, for which alkaline pancreas enzyme juices are secreted. The digestion of the proteins, however, starts in the stomach with the secretion of acidic digestive juices and continues in the duodenum, and they are absorbed in the small intestine. When carbohydrates and proteins are eaten at the same meal, both basic juices and acid juices are secreted and neutralize each other; thus neither of the essential food elements are digested.

The carbohydrates that are not digested properly reach the small intestine where there is a special bacterial flora substrate that causes fermentation. Other bacteria cause the decomposition of proteins that are not properly digested in the large intestine, or putrefaction in which process those proteins generate the secretion of nitrites that integrate into and affect the metabolic process. These materials, together with other poisons absorbed by the large intestine, poison and overburden the liver, which consequently has the task of filtering a large quantity of poisons, partially digested animal protein, and fats.

Increasing Vitality through Breathing

Breathing fresh air that contains many negative ions inhibits the natural energetic decline, improves health, and extends life.

Four main types of breathing can be discerned:

- thoracic breathing
- clavicular breathing
- diaphragmatic breathing
- full breathing

Thoracic breathing occurs because of the activity of the rib muscles, which expand the thorax upward and reduce the pressure within the lungs when inhaling air.

Clavicular breathing (raising the shoulders) appears as a result of tension, during pregnancy, or when there are pulmonary diseases, such as asthma and emphysema. Such breathing enables the lower, more expanded part of the lungs to remain motionless and thus to save it effort for the needs of blood oxygenation.

Diaphragmatic breathing is the most common type of breathing possible because of the contraction and relaxation of the diaphragm. The diaphragm is a strong and flexible muscle that separates the thorax and the stomach cavity. Adults often forget how to use it in order to breath. It acts as a pump not only for breathing but also for the functioning of the cardiovascular system. Accordingly, when one is inhaling, the diaphragm compresses the liver, the spleen, and the stomach; sends blood into the stomach and the openings; enables the return of venous blood (from the veins in the stomach cavity to the chest) to the thorax; and compresses the lymph capillaries and blood vessels of the stomach.

Full breathing is breathing that involves the thoracic muscles between the ribs, the clavicle, and the diaphragm. These improve the oxygenation and blood flow; the number of breaths per minute (relative to the number of heartbeats) drops, and considerable essential energy is saved, barely straining the heart while improving breathing ability. This breathing is facilitated by developing awareness and the ability to diagnose the different types of breathing. It should be practiced prior to meditating or relaxation exercises.

Breathing Exercise to Increase the Vitality of the Inner Organs

The following exercise allows the body to be charged with large quantities of vital energy that will reach the inner organs, the glands, and the muscles through the bloodstream and the meridians and increase cognitive ability and the ability to concentrate. The exercise can be done standing or sitting, in bed, or walking.

Empty the lungs of air. Start breathing slowly. Inhale air while expanding the nostrils.

- At the same time, imagine a stream of light flowing into and filling the lungs.
- When the lungs are full of air, concentrate on the anal muscles. Contract the external circular muscle and the pelvic floor muscle. While doing this, a strong contraction in the lower pelvis will be felt, preventing the escape of energy from the openings.
- The lower abdomen is then contracted (making a circular shape of the area below the navel) in order to create counterpressure to the diaphragm (the air is still trapped in the lungs).
- Simultaneously, the throat muscles are contracted by closing the pharynx and tilting the neck backward.

- Now after the three closures—the anus, the stomach, and the neck—swallow the saliva and imagine the energy being pushed as deep as possible into the lower stomach.
- Simultaneously, imagine the pelvis full of light and feel a warm flow in that area.
- Slowly release the three muscles and exhale the air in one long breath through the nose while keeping the tongue pressed to the upper palette. While exhaling, imagine the light spreading throughout the body.
- After a brief pause, release the muscles and repeat the exercise, at first taking three of four breaths each cycle and then increasing to seven breaths each cycle.

Three cycles of this exercise daily are recommended.

Breathing Exercise to Purify Poisons

This exercise to purify the lungs and blood of poisons is effective and important for most of the population because of polluted air. It is particularly recommended for smokers and residents of large cities. The exercise is performed seated, while keeping the shoulders loose. The tongue should be pushed hard against the upper palette, and the anal and neck muscles should be partially closed.

Exhale all the air from the lungs through the nostrils or the mouth, while strongly contracting the stomach walls.

- Inhale air up to half the lung capacity, and exhale all the air in one sharp movement without stopping.
- Repeat the action, and reach twenty breaths per minute.

This breathing should be practiced in the evening during self-energy washout (see the book *Energy an Emotion Washout*).

This exercise increases the level of oxidization and reduces the level of CO_2 in the blood, thus reducing its level of acidity and raising its level of basicity.

The strong and rhythmic contractions of the wall of the stomach cavity provide a vital massage to the internal organs and the glands, increase the oxidization of the stomach cavity; and prevent the accumulation of excess fats. They also strengthen the diaphragm and the stomach muscles. Increasing the intensity of the breathing at the same time as contraction affects the flow of blood even in the finest capillaries.

The potent exhalation of air creates strong energetic waves in the entire cardiovascular system that pass through the veins to the brain, causing it to contract and expand rhythmically. This is a type of massage of the brain cells, assisting the transfer of the cerebral fluid to all the cells, while the blood pressure remains stable despite the increased pace and volume of the flow of blood.

Sex and Vitality

The sexual connection creates important energetic dynamics whether at the main poles of the male and female or whether between the positive and negative poles of the same person, during important energetic flow along the meridians. Consequently, sexual energy feeds the inner organs. This is a process that arouses life in the whole body since it increases the hormonal and mainly the sexual secretions that fill the body with vitality and inhibit the aging process. On the other hand, while ejaculating sperm, important energy is lost through the seminal fluid. Hence, the main purpose is to increase vitality while directing the potential in the reproductive cells to encourage children in the spiritual direction of growth.

From the physical perspective, the loss of sexual energy weakens the kidneys and the adrenal gland, which are considered the key points of sexual intensity and of the body's vitality. The adrenal glands produce a variety of hormones of great importance to the diverse metabolic processes and physiological functioning. For both men and women, they also produce a small amount of the female estrogen hormone, which organizes the other secretions of the sex glands, such as the testicles, the prostate gland, and the ovaries. These affect the functioning of the pineal gland, the hypophysis, and the thyroid gland. A lack of balance between the female and the male energy in the body is liable to generate an imbalance in the sexual and hormonal energy.

Thus, for example, the secretion of the male hormone among men who lose their male energy will decline and consequently will lead to a drop in sexual drive to the point of impotence. For women, the loss of female energy will appear as indicators of an increase in the level of male energy; male hormones will be secreted and manifested in diverse ways, such as the growth of facial hair and a decrease in the size and loss of tonus of the breasts. If this is the case, our purpose is to preserve the good level of vitality on the one hand and a balance on the other hand, in order to increase the male and female hormonal secretions and to maintain their balance.

It is important to remember that the secretion of the sex hormone represents the person's energetic state. A high level of male energy will lead to the secretion of testosterone, while a high level of female energy will lead to an increase in the secretion of estrogen. Men with a surfeit of male energy have a high level of rich, viscous testosterone, which is resistant and capable of flowing, and they are immune to infections and other diseases. Men with a low level of male energy have a low level of testosterone in the blood and a small amount of delicate and watery sperm open to illness.

Regular sexual relations directly stimulate the creation of hormones that are essential to the hormonal balance. For men, sexual stimulation is one of the most efficient means to maintain the production of sex hormones and maintaining a hormonal balance; for women, sexual stimulation, menstruation, and pregnancy are important mechanisms for hormonal secretion.

With age, there is energetic loss and the battery tends to drain. However, regular sexual activity without ejaculation of sperm preserves the energy of the kidneys and of the adrenal gland and prevents the loss of hair, wrinkling of the skin, deterioration of the muscle tone, weakening of the bone marrow and the secretion of blood cells, osteoporosis, and sexual impotence and other age-connected problems.

Studies have found that frequent sexual relations between elderly partners alleviate chronic rheumatic joint pains because of stimulating the secretion of cortisones from the membrane of the adrenal gland. However, other studies have proven that such relations prevent the functioning of the adrenal gland in the male due to the ejaculation of sperm and a surfeit of energetic loss.

The Level of Vitality and the Sunlight

The fact that the body is more active and full of vitality when it is exposed to the sun is known intuitively to everyone who feels far better in spring and summer compared to the autumn and winter. It is therefore very important to listen to our body in order to assess its need for exposure to the sun's rays.

The change in the level of vitality is felt not only in the change in the seasons but also in the transition from day to night. Experiments conducted on animals intended to determine a fatal dose of radiation prove that a larger dose of fatal medication is needed during the day than at night, testifying to the fact that the sun's natural rays can reduce the negative effect of poisonous materials.

The sunlight has a proven effect on the secretion of the male hormone testosterone and the female hormone progesterone. Reduced exposure of the eyes to the sun, as in cases of cataract or blindness, is accompanied by a decline in the level of testosterone in the blood.[89]

The symptoms of a low level of testosterone in the blood are identical to those of a decline in the level of vitality, as, for example, a decline in sexual desire, a decline in the number of sperm cells or their nonproduction, general weakness, muscular dystrophy, anemia, osteoporosis, weight gain, depression, and other symptoms.

Sunlight raises the level of the growth hormone (HGH) in the blood and affects the pace of development of the embryo during the last stages of pregnancy and during the first stages of the infant's development.[91] The journal *Nature* published a study conducted in Austria over the last ten years on more than five hundred thousand people that explored a possible connection between the month of birth and the child's height. It proved that children born in the months when exposure to sunlight is greater are taller than those born in months when the exposure to sunlight is less. The tallest were born in April, while the shortest were born in October. This is explained as the sunlight increasing the secretion of the growth hormone.[90]

The real problem of many people nowadays stems from the fact that they spend far more time in buildings, in a closed place lit by artificial light lacking ultraviolet rays, attached to the television and the computer, eating artificial food without vitality, causing weight gain and future health problems.

Based on many scientific studies, one can summarize the benefit of regular and controlled exposure to the sun's rays. It:

- improves the tolerance to emotional tension and the emotional state
- lowers the level of cholesterol in the blood
- increases the secretion of the male testosterone hormone and the female progesterone hormone
- reduces aggressive behavior
- improves the effectiveness of the immune system
- increases physical ability
- improves the mental perception and increases the ability to understand
- causes the secretion of vitamin D needed for the absorption of calcium and minerals, reduces dental caries, and improves osteoporosis
- charges the body with energy after illness or exertion

- prevents bacterial proliferation and the development of infectious illnesses
- improves the flow of blood in the skin, which becomes more flexible and resilient to infectious illnesses
- affects esthetics (sun tanning)
- reduces sleep disturbances and organizes the biological clock
- increases the sex drive and fertility
- improves arthritis
- improves sight
- regulates menstruation and the hormonal cycle
- increases the growth process
- reduces the desire for alcohol and drugs and reduces dependency on them
- reduces the chances of the development of cancerous growths, including skin cancer

Therefore, various steps are recommended, including controlled exposure to sunlight in all seasons, equipping oneself with home lamps that also diffuse ultraviolet rays; eating healthy, fresh food so that the sun's light has a positive effect; drinking fruit and vegetable juices; taking vitamins, especially A, E, and C; eating fresh tomatoes with olive oil; gradual exposure to the sun but not for extended periods of time; avoiding the use of protective creams that include chemicals as far as possible (instead of smearing them on it is preferable to limit the length of exposure); restricting the use of sunglasses to let the eyes benefit from the effect of the ultraviolet rays; taking the children out to play in the open air; sitting outdoors during pregnancy, especially close to the birth and also thereafter, possibly in the shade; painting children's rooms in yellows and oranges in order to raise their level of concentration and learning ability, and allowing them to eat fresh food and avoid industrialized sweets.

The way to know the correct amount of exposure to the sun is by avoiding phenomena such as redness, itching, burning, and pain due to exaggerated exposure to the light, a level we would not recommend reaching.

The Signs of Healthy Person
with Good Vitality

A healthy person with a good level of vitality, who does not suffer from excess tension, will have:

- an erect body and relaxed and strong muscles, without difficulty contracting or relaxing them
- a pink-tanned skin color, warm and rich in blood, perspiring hot sweat and enjoying touch
- a lively facial expression with a slight smile, without puckering his or her eyes, corners of his or her mouth straight or tending slightly upward, full pink lips, damp mouth mucous, easily producing saliva with no difficulty swallowing and no need of additional liquids in order to swallow solid food

In this person:

- The eyes shine, as if speaking and are open wide; the eyeball is not prominent or too recessed; the pupils react to light.
- Breathing is full, deep, and slow and includes a slight pause after exhaling; the rate is uniform, involving the chest and diaphragm. Inhalation is full with a feeling of relish that reaches the sex organs.
- The heart beats peacefully, and the pulse is calm and full; blood pressure is normal.

- The stomach is soft and bowel movements regular; feces have volume and are semisolid; the excretion of gasses is sparse with no smell of rotting.
- Women have a regular monthly period. The color of the blood is red and full of life; the breasts are full; touching the nipples will cause a rapid sexual stimulus, with a rich secretion of vaginal lubricating fluid. The orgasmic contractions are regular and pleasurable for the whole body with a feeling of physical languidness and emotional release after orgasm.
- The erogenous areas of men, including the nipples, are sensitive and fully erect after slight sexual stimulation. The orgasmic contractions involve the whole body and are accompanied by the ejection of a normal quantity of seminal fluid. The mood is good, loving, and giving without difficulty; the flexibility of the system causes a man to be relaxed and tolerant. The intensity of the inner energy provides immunity from criticism or external attack.

The homeostatic mechanism regulates the defense system in order to cope with the continuing changes therein. Every bipolar system functions in a similar manner, whether it is an animal or not. The external stimuli alter the basic energetic frequency that maintains the homeostasis. An emotional crisis, electromagnetic radiation, or physical trauma can alter the basic frequency of part or all of the animal soul's magnetic field. Such a change can alter the functioning and structure of the affected part in a way that is not compatible with its role in the entire system. However, if the defense mechanism functions well, it intervenes immediately, returns the original frequency, and maintains the homeostasis.

The defense system is actually the vitality of the system. It tries ceaselessly to maintain a dynamic balance with minimal energetic investment. Therefore, a person who behaves emotionally and physically according to his or her natural makeup will flow with the stream and will feel he or she applies his or her ambitions. He or she will live in physical, emotional, and spiritual well-being.

Lack of Energy and Vital Exhaustion

A lack of energy results from the ongoing loss of emotional energy due to extended emotional crises, inner extended conflict, eating food lacking vitality, exaggerated physical work, few hours of sleep, and isolation without support or outside help.

The signs indicating a decline in the level of vitality and the draining of "batteries" are:

- general weakness; a twisted and weak spine; lackluster, dry, grayish skin and sunken dry eyes; extended pupils that react slowly to light; and a lack of perspiration
- a distant look, slack facial and jaw muscles, slightly blue lips, a dry mouth that does not secrete saliva, difficulty digesting due to a decline in the secretion of digestive enzyme, anemia
- slow, shallow breathing
- slow heart rate, with a short and shallow pulse; low blood pressure; dizziness

In this person:

- The muscles are flaccid and lack tension and are covered with a thick layer of fat.
- The stomach is soft; there is a lack of stomach acidity, difficulty digesting, and constipation.

- Low sexual drive causes a significant decline in sexual desire. Women suffer from vaginal dryness, menstruation ceases, and there is an inability to reach orgasm. Men suffer from difficulty attaining or maintaining an erection; a brief orgasm accompanied by pain in the area of the prostate gland and the rectum, a bad feeling after orgasm that is characterized by emptiness and a lack of desire to make and create (depression following orgasm).

The appearance of cancerous growths is an extreme situation of the loss of vitality in a particular organ or throughout the body. All the illnesses that appear as overflaccidity, such as muscular weakness, hiatus hernia, hernia, prolapsed womb, varicose veins in the legs, a weak heart muscle, and a drop in blood pressure point to a lack of energy. From the emotional perspective, this is manifested in depression, the need to sleep, difficulty getting up in the morning, and disinterest in performing. Among children, it appears as restlessness, lack of concentration, hyperactivity, fear, and anxiety.

The loss of vital energy leads to vital exhaustion, and it is defined as feelings of depression, decreased vigor, and increased fatigue. It has previously been investigated mainly as a risk factor for cardiovascular disease and cancer. It has three defining characteristics: (1) feelings of excessive fatigue and lack of energy, (2) increasing irritability, and (3) feelings of demoralization.[92]

It has been suggested that vital exhaustion (VE) is a mental state at which people arrive when their resources for adapting to stress are broken down. The concept of vital exhaustion grew out of an interest in understanding the mental state of "undue fatigue" and "lack of energy."

Vital exhaustion is an extreme lack of energy that can cause pathophysiological disturbances, such as increased levels of insulin and C-peptide in response to glucose challenge and with an enhanced insulin-to-glucose ratio in middle-aged healthy men; furthermore, it correlates with abdominal obesity in those men having a low body mass index and deficient fibrinolysis.[93]

The metabolic changes associated with vital exhaustion may be attributable to sympathetic, adrenomedullary, and hypothalamic-pituitary-adrenocortical system alterations. It has been demonstrated that a decrease of basal cortisol and a compensatory increase of basal andrenocortiotropic hormone (ACTH) secretion, as well as an increased ratio of 17-hydorxyprogesterone (17-OHP) to 11-deoxycortisol and an increase of cortisol to ACTH stimulation are among the pituitary-adrenocortical alterations associated with the hyperinulinemia, dyslipidemia, and abdominal obesity components of the insulin resistance syndrome.[94]

Treating a Lack of Energy

In cases of a lack of energy, we recommend:

- avoiding aggressive physical activity
- avoiding isolation and excessive crying
- avoiding long showers, baths, or swimming in a pool
- avoiding drinking alcohol or drugs
- reducing the time spent sitting at the computer
- reducing sexual relations and avoiding the use of artificial means to achieve erection (such as Viagra, Cialis, injections into the penis for erection, or implanting a prosthesis)
- increasing the ingestion of fresh fruit and vegetable juices and avoiding eating "empty calories"
- coffee enemas (see the energy and emotion washout book)
- sleeping many hours at night
- charging through energetic energy and emotion washout

The presence of loving people and support and love afford the most important means to handle children and people with a low level of vitality.

In Conclusion

We live in a very important period—the period of transition to a new scientific model that will affect all areas of science from physics through biology to medicine, a shift from Newtonian mechanics to Einstein's energy model and Reich to the Chinese model to the quantum mechanics.

The key factor in the application of medicine these days is the shortage of time. Physicians must treat the patient in a very short time and with high efficiency, as the patient wishes to receive treatment without having to spend his or her time in vain. This is why doctors and patients alike prefer pills or surgical operation to the implementation of major changes in lifestyle.

Desperate attempts to find a quick solution to the symptoms indicate, without a doubt, the lack of responsibility. Western society dictates an energetic lifestyle at a breakneck pace. Ensuring proper nutrition and exercise are often perceived as a task to be added to an already busy schedule. Most people prefer to eat to satiety, drink alcohol to improve mood, and enjoy idleness and inactivity after a long and exhausting day.

There is no doubt that in recent years we have witnessed a change of attitudes toward disease. People seek alternative ways to solve health problems that were not resolved in conventional methods. The increasing use of CAM in the official institutes is due to patient demand, and there is evidence that patients frequently use more than one modality of medical care. More people are turning to these treatments. Hospitals have opened departments for unconventional medical treatments and therapies. HMOs finance acupuncture, homeopathy, reflexology, and more. That pattern will probably continue and may even expand as evidence of treatment effectiveness accumulates. Health care that integrates CAM therapies with conventional medicine has been termed "integrative medicine" by many.

This book presents a model whereby disease is a process that indicates an imbalance in the body, resulting from an imbalance of vital energy due to mental and emotional distress. We therefore consider disease as a warning sign, announcing that psychological conflict has not been resolved and learning potential has been disrupted. Behind every psychological conflict there is potential for change, consciousness expansion, and spiritual evolution. Treating symptoms is just like covering the LED in the car that indicates the lack of oil or fuel. It is obvious that treating or ignoring the warning light will not solve the real problem. If we do not go to the root of the problem, we just convert the disease into a chronic one with all the consequences.

Disease has therefore a clear purpose: to guide the person to change his or her lifestyle. As the disease gets its purpose, the person learns to change and evolve; there is no longer a need for the disease.

Today's leading medical model treats disease as the result of external factors that cause discomfort, so illnesses are attributed to physical trauma, poisoning, and infections. In recent years, Western medicine has begun to attribute more importance to some psychological stressors, but it is still done in general and undefined way.

The content of this book is a continuation of the first book "the Seven Principles and the Seventh Sense". The proposed method in this book is unique in that it clearly defines the relationship between emotional crisis and the affected organ; in addition, we understand the relation between the emotional expression and the type of disease in the specific organ, the modality of conflict perception, and the embryologic layer in that organ.

Identification of the crisis is the important first step in the healing process. Through the seventh sense, anyone who can learn and develop can not only detect the background emotional crisis of physical disorder but also identify the year it took place and stand on its origin. This kind of interaction with the patient creates a deep spiritual and psychological bridge between the patient and the therapist.

This approach is significantly different from the accepted approach in conventional medicine. We are responsible for our health and disease. The disease is a kind of test, which aims to deepen our experience, expand our consciousness, and help us take a step further in our spiritual evolution. The healing process is, therefore, a developmental process that leads the oppressive human mental barrier to spiritual liberation, giving deep satisfaction and happiness.

According to this model, future doctors play an important role in changing the perception of the disease and modifying its settings. Pure spirit, patience, and love will be the guidelines of future doctors.

Complete health will be reflected in a full balance between mind, body, and soul, and a complete physical, psychological, and social well-being will be obtained. In this state, the patient will be able to realize his or her objects in life with a sense of love, happiness, and freedom.

Love is the way.

Happiness is the sign.

Light is the purpose; from the light we came, to the light we will come back.

References

1. National health expenditures aggregate, per capita amounts, percent distribution, and average annual percent growth, by source of funds: selected calendar years 1960–2007 [Internet]. Baltimore, MD: Centers for Medicare and Medicaid Services; 2008. Available from: http://www.cms.hhs.gov/NationalHealthExpendData/downloads/tables.pdf.

2. Alternative Medicine. (1999). "Exploring Your Treatment Options." *International Health News*, 93.

3. Maizes, V., and O. Caspio. (1999). "The Principles and Challenges of Alternative Medicine: More than a Combination of Traditional and Alternative Therapies." *West J Med* 171: 148–149.

4. Bates, D. W., et al. (1995). "Incidence of Adverse Drug Events and Potential Adverse Drug Events." *Journal of the American Medical Association* 274, 29–34.

5. Lazarou, J., et al. (1998). "Incidence of Adverse Drug Reactions in Hospitalized Patients." *Journal of the American Medical Association* 279: 1200–1205; 1216–1217. (Editorial).

6. Roach, G. W., et al. (1996). "Adverse Cerebral Outcomes after Coronary Bypass Surgery." *New England Journal of Medicine* 335: 1857–63.

7. Murray, M. T. (1996). *Encyclopedia of Nutritional Supplements* (Rocklin, CA: Prima Publishing).

8. Moghadasian, M. H., et al. (1997). "Homocysteine and Coronary Artery Disease." *Archives of Internal Medicine* 157: 2299–2308.

9. Perry, I. J., et al. (1995). "Prospective Study of Serum Total Homocysteine Concentration and Risk of Stroke in Middle-Aged British Men." *The Lancet* 346: 1395–1398.

10. "Lowering Blood Homocysteine with Folic Acid Based Supplements: Meta-Analysis of Randomized Trials." *British Medical Journal* 316: 894–898.

11. Clarke, R., et al. (1998). "Folate, Vitamin B12, and Serum Total Homocysteine Levels in Confirmed Alzheimer's Disease." *Archives of Neurology* 55: 1449–1455 and 1407–1408. (Editorial).

12. Wilt, T. J., et al. (1998). "Saw Palmetto Extracts for Treatment of Benign Prostatic Hyperplasia." *Journal of the American Medical Association* 280: 1604–1609.

13. Austin, J. A. (1998). "Why Patients Use Alternative Medicine." *JAMA* 279: 1548–1553; Lewith, G. T. (1998). "Reflections on the Nature of Consultation." *J Altern Complement Med* 4: 321–323.

14. Barnes, P., E. Powell-Griner, K. McFann, and R. Nahin. (2002). *CDC Advance Data Report #343. Complementary and Alternative Medicine Use among Adults* (United States).

15. "The Mainstreaming of Alternative Medicine." (2000). *Consumer Reports*, 17–21.

16. Eisenberg DM· et al. 1998. Trends in alternative medicine use in the United States, 1990-1997: results of a follow-up national survey. *JAMA*, Nov. 1998, 220, 1575–1569.

17. FSMB (Federation of State Medical Boards). (2002). *Model Guidelines for the Use of Complementary and Alternative Therapies in Medical Practice.* (Dallas, TX: Federation of State Medical Boards).

18. http://www.who.int/mediacentre/news/releases/2004/pr44/en/index.html.

19. Eisenberg, D. M., R. B. Davis, S. L. Ettner, et al. (1998). "Unconventional Medicine in the US: Prevalence, Costs, and Patterns of Use." *JAMA* 290: 1569–1575.

20. Association of American Medical Colleges Medical School Objectives Project. (1998). *Report I: Learning Objectives for Medical Student Education: Guidelines for Medical Schools* (Washington DC);

21. Mitchell, A., and M. Cormack. (1998). *The Therapeutic Relationship in Complementary Health Care*. Edinburgh: Churchill Livingstone.

22. Eisenberg, D. M., R. B. Davis, S. L. Ettner, et al. (1998). "Unconventional Medicine in the US: Prevalence, Costs, and Patterns of Use." *JAMA* 290: 1569–1575;

23. Moore, J., K. Phipps, D. Marcer, and G. Lewith. (1985). "Why Do People Seek Treatment by Alternative Medicine?" *British Medical Journal* 290 no. 1: 28–29.

24. Patel, K. (1999). "Physicians for the 21st Century: Challenges Facing Medical Education in the United States." *Evaluation and the Health Professions* 22: 379–398.

25. Oshry, Barry (2008). *Seeing Systems: Unlocking the Mysteries of Organizational Life.*

26. Berrett-Koehler; Auyang, Sunny Y. (1999). *Foundations of Complex-System Theories: In Economics, Evolutionary Biology, and Statistical Physics*, Cambridge University Press.

27. Eisenberg, D. M., R. B. Davis, S. L. Ettner, et al. (1998). "Unconventional Medicine in the US: Prevalence, Costs, and Patterns of Use." *JAMA* 290: 1569–1575.

28. Bensoussan, A., and G. T. Lewith. (2004). "Complementary Medicine Research in Australia: A Strategy for the Future." *MJA* 181, no. 6: 331–333.

29. Kleijnen, J., A. J. de Craen, J. van Everdingen, and L. Krol. (1994). "Placebo Effect in Double-Blind Clinical Trials: A Review of Interactions with Medications." *The Lancet* 344: 1347–1349.

30. Nadeau, R., and M. Kafatos. (1999). *The Non-Local Universe: The New Physics and Matters of the Mind* (Oxford, UK: Oxford University Press).

31. Kamien, Roger (2008). *Music: An Appreciation*, 6th Brief Edition, p.41. ISBN 978-0-07-340134-8.

32. Bohm, D., and B. J. Hiley. (1975). "On the Intuitive Understanding of Nonlocality as Implied by Quantum Theory." *Foundations of Physics*, Volume 5, Number 1, 93–109. DOI: 10.1007/BF01100319.

33. B. J. Hiley. *"Information, Quantum Theory and the Brain."* In Gordon G. Globus (ed.), Karl H. Pribram (ed.), and Giuseppe Vitiello (ed.).

"Brain and Being: At the Boundary between Science, Philosophy, Language and Arts, Advances in Consciousness Research" (John Benjamins B.V., 2004), 197–214.

34. Pratt, David. (1993). "David Bohm and the Implicate Order." Appeared in: *Sunrise* magazine, February/March 1993 (Theosophical University Press).

35. Stipanuk, M. A. *Biochemical and Physiological Aspects of Human Nutrition* (Philadelphia, PA: W. B. Saunders Company, 2000).

36. Becker, R. O. *Cross Currents* (London, England: Bloomsbury Publishing, 1990); Becker, R.O., and G. Selden. *The Body Electric* (New York: W. Morrow and Company Inc, 1985).

37. Bortner, C. D., and J. A. Cidlowski. (2004). "The Role of Apoptotic Volume Decrease and Ionic Homeostasis in the Activation and Repression of Apoptosis." *Pflugers Archiv* 448: 313–318.

38. Franco, R., C. D. Bortner, and J. A. Cidlowski. (2006). "Potential Roles of Electrogenic Ion Transport and Plasma Membrane Depolarization in Apoptosis." *Journal of Membrane Biology* 209: 43–58.

39. Binggeli, R., and R. C. Weinstein. (1986). "Membrane Potentials and Sodium Channels: Hypotheses for Growth Regulation and Cancer Formation Based on Changes in Sodium Channels and Gap Junctions." *Journal of Theoretical Biology* 123: 377–401.

40. Binggeli, R., and R. C. Weinstein. (1986). "Membrane Potentials and Sodium Channels: Hypotheses for Growth Regulation and Cancer Formation Based on Changes in Sodium Channels and Gap Junctions." *Journal of Theoretical Biology* 123: 377–401.

41. Cone, C. D., Jr. (1971). "Unified Theory on the Basic Mechanism of Normal Mitotic Control and Oncogenesis." *Journal of Theoretical Biology* 30: 151–181.

42. Presman, A. S. "Electromagnetic Fields and Life" (New York, NY: Plenum Press, 1970).

43. Winterfeld, H. J., et al. (1993). "Effects of Sauna Therapy on Patients with Coronary Heart Disease with Hypertension after Bypass Operation after Heart Aneurism Operation and Essential Hypertension." *Z Gesamte Inn Med* 48: 247–250.

44. Ibid.

45. Kihara, T., S. Biro, M. Imamura, et al. (2002). "Repeated Sauna Treatment Improves Vascular Endothelial and Cardiac Function in Patients with Chronic Heart Failure" 39: 254–259.

46. Laitinen, L. A., et al. (1989). "Lungs and Ventilation in Sauna." *Ann Clin Res* 20: 244–248;

47. Cox, N. J. M., et al. (1988). "Sauna Transiently Improve Pulmonary Function in Patients with Obstructive Lung Disease." *Arch Phys Med Rehabil* 70: 911–913.

48. Isomaki, H. (1988). "The Sauna and Rheumatic Disease." *Ann Clin Res* 20: 271–275.

49. Goldfarb, A. H. (1999). "Nutritional Antioxidants as Therapeutic and Preventive Modalities in Exercise-Induced Muscle Damage." *Can. J. Appl. Physiol.* 24: 249–266.

50. *Journal of the American Medical Association* (*JAMA*), June 2002.

51. Sebastian, A., L. A. Frassetto, D. E. Sellmeyer, R. L. Merriam, and R. C. Morris, Jr. (2002). "Estimation of the Net Acid Load of the Diet of Ancestral Pre-Agricultural *Homo sapiens* and their hominid ancestors." *Am J Clin Nutr.* 76 no. 6: 1308–16.

52. Frasssetto, et al. (2001). *Eur. J. Nutr.* 40 no. 5: 200–213.

53. Frassetto, L., and A. J. Sebastian. (1996). "Gerontol A." *Biol Sci Med Sci.* 51 no. 1: B91 33;-30, 32-;

54. Longeran, E.T. (1988). *Geriatrics,* 43 no. 3: 27, 520).-2253).62(2): 511-;

55. Nabata, T., et al. (1992). *Nippon Rinsho* 50 no 9: 2249.

56. Wiederkehr, M., and R. Krapf. (2001). "Metabolic and Endocrine Effects of Metabolic Acidosis in Humans." *Swiss Med Wkly.* 131 no. 9–10: 127–32.

57. Brungger, M., H. N. Hulter, and R. Krapf. (1997). "Effect of Chronic Metabolic Acidosis on the Growth Hormone/IGF-1 Endocrine Axis: New Cause of Growth Hormone Insensitivity in Humans." *Kidney Int.* 51 no. 1: 216–21;

58. Challa, A., W. Chan, R. J. Krieg, Jr., M. A. Thabet, F. Liu, R. L. Hintz, and J. C. Chan. (1993). "Effect of Metabolic Acidosis on the Expression of Insulin-like Growth Factor and Growth Hormone Receptor." *Kidney Int.* 44 no. 6: 1224–7.

59. Kuemmerle, N., R. J. Krieg, Jr., K. Latta, A. Challa, J. D. Hanna, and J. C. Chan. (1997). "Growth Hormone and Insulin-like Growth Factor in Non-Uremic Acidosis and Uremic Acidosis." *Kidney Int Suppl.* 58: S102–105.

60. Challa, A., W. Chan, R. J. Krieg, Jr., M. A. Thabe, F. Liu, R. L. Hintz, and J. C. Chan. (1993). "Effect of Metabolic Acidosis on the Expression of Insulin-like Growth Factor and Growth Hormone Receptor." *Kidney Int.* 44 no. 6: 1224–7. (See endnote 13.)

61. Mahlbacher, K., A. Sicuro, H. Gerber, H. N. Hulter, and R. Krapf. (1999). "Growth Hormone Corrects Acidosis-Induced Renal Nitrogen Wasting and Renal Phosphate Depletion and Attenuates Renal Magnesium Wasting in Humans." *Metabolism* 48 no. 6: 763–70.

62. Challa, A., R. J. Krieg, Jr., M. A. Thabet, J. D. Veldhuis, and J. C. Chan. (1993). "Metabolic Acidosis Inhibits Growth Hormone Secretion in Rats: Mechanism of Growth Retardation." *Am J Physiol.* Oct. 265 no. 4, Pt 1: E547–53.

63. Sutton, J. R., N. L. Jones, and C. J. Toews. (1976). "Growth Hormone Secretion in Acid-Base Alterations at Rest and during Exercise." *Clin Sci Mol Med.* 50 no. 4: 241–247.

64. Wiederkehr, M., and R. Krapf. (2001). "Metabolic and Endocrine Effects of Metabolic Acidosis in Humans." *Swiss Med Wkly* 131 no. 9–10: 127–132.

65. Brungger, M., H. N. Hulter, and R. Krapf. (1997). "Effect of Chronic Metabolic Acidosis on Thyroid Hormone Homeostasis in Humans." *Am J Physiol* 272: 648–653.

66. Wiederkehr, M., and R. Krapf. (2001). "Metabolic and Endocrine Effects of Metabolic Acidosis in Humans." *Swiss Med Wkly* 131 no. 9–10: 127–132.

67. Maurer, M., W. Riesen, J. Muser, H. N. Hulter, and R. Krapf. (2003). "Neutralization of Western Diet Inhibits Bone Resorption Independently of K Intake and Reduces Cortisol Secretion in Humans." *Am J Physiol Renal Physiol.* 284 no. 1: 32–40. Epub Sep 24, 2002.

68. Welbourne, T. C. (1989). "Glucocorticoid and Acid-Base Homeostasis: Effects on Glutamine Metabolism and Transport." *Am J Kidney Dis.* 14 no. 4: 293–7.

69. May, R. C., J. L. Bailey, W. E. Mitch, T. Masud, and B. K. England. (1996). "Glucocorticoids and Acidosis Stimulate Protein and Amino Acid Catabolism In Vivo." *Kidney Int.* 49 no. 3: 679–83.

70. Price, S. R., B. K. England, J. L. Bailey, K. Van Vreede, and W. E. Mitch. (1994). "Acidosis and Glucocorticoids Concomitantly Increase Ubiquitin and Proteasome Subunit mRNAs in Rat Muscle." *Am J Physiol.* 267: 955–960.

71. Barefoot, R. R., and C. J. Reich. *The Calcium Factor: The Scientific Secret of Health and Youth.*

72. New SA. Nutrition Society Medal lecture. (2002). "The Role of the Skeleton in Acid-Base Homeostasis." *Proc Nutr Soc.* 2: 151–64.

73. Wiederkehr, M., and R. Krapf. (2001). "Metabolic and Endocrine Effects of Metabolic Acidosis in Humans." *Swiss Med Wkly.* 131 no. 9–10: 127–132.

74. Buclin, T., M. Cosma, M. Appenzeller, A. F. Jacquet, L. A. Decosterd, J. Biollaz, and P. Burckhardt. (2001). "Diet Acids and Alkalis Influence Calcium Retention in Bone." *Osteoporos Int.* 12 no. 6: 493–499.

75. Price, S. R., B. K. England, J. L. Bailey, K. Van Vreede, and W. E. Mitch. (1994). "Acidosis and Glucocorticoids Concomitantly Increase Ubiquitin and Proteasome Subunit mRNAs in Rat Muscle." *Am J Physiol.* 267: 955–960.

76. Wachman, A., and D. S. Bernstein. (1968). "Diet and Osteoporosis." *The Lancet* 4 no. 1: 958–959.

77. Caudarella, R., F. Vescini, A. Buffa, G. La Manna, and S. Stefoni. (2004). "Osteoporosis and Urolithiasis." *Urol Int.* 72 Suppl 1: 17–19.

78. New SA. Nutrition Society Medal lecture. (2002). "The Role of the Skeleton in Acid-Base Homeostasis." *Proc Nutr Soc.* 61 no. 2: 151–164.

79. Tylavsky, F. A., K. Holliday, R. Danish, C. Womack, J. Norwood, and L. Carbone. (2004). "Fruit and Vegetable Intakes Are an

Independent Predictor of Bone Size in Early Pubertal Children." *American Journal of Clinical Nutrition* 79 no. 2: 311–317.

80. Welbourne, T. C. (1980). "Acid-Base Balance and Plasma Glutamine Concentration in Man." *Eur J Appl Physiol Occup Physiol.* 45 no. 2–3: 185–188.

81. Welbourne, T. C., V. Phromphetcharat, G. Givens, and S. Joshi. (1986). "Regulation of Interorganal Glutamine Flow in Metabolic Acidosis." *Am J Physiol.* 250: 457–463.

82. Ballmer, P. E., M. A. McNurlan, H. N. Hulter, S. E. Anderson, P. J. Garlick, and R. Krapf. (1995). "Chronic Metabolic Acidosis Decreases Albumin Synthesis and Induces Negative Nitrogen Balance in Humans." *J Clin Invest.* 95 no. 1: 39–45.

83. Caso, G., B. A. Garlick, G. A. Casella, D. Sasvary, and P. J. Garlick. (2004). "Acute Metabolic Acidosis Inhibits Muscle Protein Synthesis in Rats." *Am J Physiol Endocrinol Metab.* 287 no. 1: 90–96. Epub February 24, 2004.

84. Mitch, W. E., and S. R. Price. (2001). "Mechanisms Activated by Kidney Disease and the Loss of Muscle Mass." *Am J Kidney Dis.* 38 no. 6: 1337–1342.

85. May, R. C., J. L. Bailey, W. E. Mitch, T. Masud, and B. K. England. (1996). "Glucocorticoids and Acidosis Stimulate Protein and Amino Acid Catabolism In Vivo." *Kidney Int.* 49 no. 3: 679–683.

86. Mitch, W. E. (1996). "Metabolic Acidosis Stimulates Protein Metabolism in Uremia." *Miner Electrolyte Metab.* 22 no. 1–3: 62–65.

87. Maizes, V., C. Schneider, I. Bell, and A. Weil. (2002). "Integrative Medical Education: Development and Implementation of a Comprehensive Curriculum at the University of Arizona." *Acad Med.* 77 no. 9: 851–860.

88. Berndtson, K. (1998). "Complementary and Alternative Medicine. Integrative Medicine: Business Risks and Opportunities." *Physician Exec.* 24 no. 6: 22–25.

89. Cortes-Gallegos, V., I. Sojo Aranda, and R. M. Gio Pelaez. (1998). "Disturbing the Light-Darkness Pattern Reduces Circulating Testosterone in Healthy Men." *Arch Androl* 40 no. 2: 129–132.

90. Weber, G. W., H. Prossenger, H. Seidler. (1998). "Depends on Month of Birth." *Nature* 391: 754–755.

91. Hobday, R. (1999). *The Healing Sun: Sunlight and Health in the 21ˢᵗ Century* (Findhorn, Scotland, and Tallahasse, FL: The Findhorn Press).

92. Appels, A., and P. Mulder. (1998a). "Excess Fatigue as a Precursor of Myocardial Infarction." *Eur Heart J* 9, 758–764.

93. Raikkonen, K., A. Hautanen, and L. Keltikangas-Jarvinen. (1994). "Association of Stress and Depression with Regional Fat Distribution in Healthy Middle-Aged Men." *J Behav Med* 17, 605–616.

94. Hautanen, A., K. Raikkonen, and H. Adlercreutz. (1997). "Associations between Pituitary-Adrenocortical Function and Abdominal Obesity, Hyperinsulinemia and Dyslipidemia in Normotensive Males." *J Intern Med*, 241, 451–461.

About the Book

Today's leading medical model treats disease as the result of external factors that cause discomfort, so illnesses are attributed to physical trauma, poisoning, and infections. In recent years, Western medicine has begun to attribute more importance to some psychological stressors, but it is still done in general and undefined ways.

People have begun seeking alternative ways to solve health problems by increasing their use of CAM, and more people are turning to these treatments. Hospitals have opened departments, and unconventional medical treatments and therapies are being financed by HMOs, including acupuncture, homeopathy, reflexology, and more. Most CAMs are based on the concept that there is an energy imbalance that should be fixed; however, they do not repair the cause of this imbalance, which is the psychological conflict.

This book presents a model whereby disease is a process that indicates an imbalance in the body, resulting from an imbalance of vital energy due to mental and emotional distress. We, therefore, consider the disease as a warning sign, announcing that psychological conflicts are not resolved and learning potential has been disrupted. Disease has a clear purpose: to guide the person to change his or her lifestyle. As the disease gets its purpose, the person learns to change and evolve; there is then no longer a need for the disease.

The disease is a kind of test that aims to deepen our experience, expand our consciousness, and help us take a step further in our spiritual evolution.

The healing process is therefore a developmental process that leads the oppressive human mental barrier to spiritual liberation, giving deep satisfaction and happiness, helping people to achieve complete well-being as defined by the World Health Organization.

About the Author

Dr. Nader Butto born in Nazareth, Israel. He graduated from medical school in Torino, Italy, in 1983, completed his cardiology specialization in Israel in 1992, and in 1995, completed his training in advanced invasive cardiology in France. Presently he is working in the Rabin Medical Center, his main work at the hospital is invasive cardiology and coronary angioplasty. Since medical school, Dr. Butto has emphasized the importance of the spiritual aspect and has been drawn toward holistic medicine. After specializing in cardiology, he has continued to seek knowledge that will fill the gaps of conventional medicine.

He developed a new theory, unified universal theory, which based on seven universal principles to describe the physical, energetic, and spiritual realms in a single unified theory.

In his outpatient clinic, he treats a wide spectrum of disorders that are considered incurable using conventional medicine. He developed a new diagnostic method based on the seventh sense as extrasensory perception by which he can find the direct relationship between the emotional crises, energetic blockages, and physical illnesses.

He has developed new therapeutic methods that combine the three different and related aspects of the human being: psyche, soul, and body—which are FEEL (fast emotional elaboration and liberation), TTRT (transtemporal regression technique), and EEW (energy emotion wash-out). The purpose of these techniques to free the body from physical ailments, elaborate the emotional crises to complete the learning process, and permit personal fulfillment and spiritual evolution.

Over the past few years, Dr. Butto has been giving lectures and practical workshops to psychologists, physicians, and therapists on his method, unified integrative medicine, in Israel, Italy, and Spain Germany, Switzerland. In October 1998, his book first was published in Italy, where it became a best seller since 1999. Since then, he has published four more books in Italian and Hebrew.

You may visit *www.naderbutto.com* for more information.

CPSIA information can be obtained
at www.ICGtesting.com
Printed in the USA
LVOW12s0221060218
565469LV00001B/52/P